# It Started with a Pickle Crock

# It Started with a Pickle Crock

**Bruce Shaffer**

Goathouse Publishing

First Printing, 2024

This book is a memoir. It reflects the author's recollection of experiences. Some events were compressed and some dialogue was recreated. Characters in the *Unfinished Stories* chapter have no existence outside the imagination of the author and have no relation to anyone bearing the same name or names. Any resemblance to individuals known or unknown to the author are purely coincidental.

Goathouse Publishing books can be ordered through bookstores or at bshafferforty9@gmail.com

Stock photo credits go to Flickr, iStock, Pexels, and Pixabay

ISBN: 979-8-8691-7380-5

# ON THE COVER

That's me (clockwise): newborn, 1st grade, 2nd grade, 3rd grade, 4th grade, 5th grade, 6th grade, 8th grade, 10th grade, 12th grade, 40 years old, and 58 years old. My parents, Judy and Jack Shaffer, are at the center of the pickle crock.

# DEDICATION

For Mom and Dad, who brought me into this world and showed me the way.

# ACKNOWLEDGEMENT

A special thanks to my wife Karen for mustering the energy to read my manuscript— twice! Her edits and additions are the defibrillator that brings many of my stories to life. Also, a big thanks to my friend Pete Springer, a retired teacher and promising new author who provided me with praise, encouragement, and valuable comments on the manuscript.

# Contents

# PROLOGUE

Dave Barry is my literary idol. Any of the humorist's anecdotes will have me busting my gut and spotting my shorts in no time. His colonoscopy anecdote was so hilarious and clever it gave me the intestinal fortitude to share the risqué subject matter with my coworkers. His David Beckham anecdote scored repeatedly and inspired me to strive for my own literary goals.

By writing *It Started with a Pickle Crock* I'm now his competitor, albeit a very lame one over which he won't lose any sleep. I can only hope some residual laughs are out there from which I can profit. I didn't profit from my premiere novella, *The Man with the Yellowfin Tuna*, a self-published crime thriller. It grossed about five bucks and netted me, well, let's just say it gave me the opportunity to claim a tax deduction come April 15.

As you can see from above, I'm not very good at marketing. I've promoted Dave Barry and slammed myself. I tend to be self-deprecating, but I think I have enough funny stories in my life to turn a profit. If so, my esteemed publisher is sending me royalty checks for writing *It Started with a Pickle Crock* and I'm sipping fine imported beer poolside. If not, I've self-published again and am swigging something much cheaper and stiffer.

So, on to the book. In it I take a look at my life, using embarrassing pictures of myself and others whenever possible. As the book title states, *It Started with a Pickle Crock . . .* my life that is. You see, Mom was very pregnant with me and was inadvisably moving a heavy clay pickle crock in the garage, unpacking from the big move to our new house. She felt a twinge and soon was in labor with me a full month early. I was a small 8-month baby, a shade over 6 pounds.

I've grown into an average-sized man, 5 feet 11 inches and 175 pounds, but I have a few peculiarities which I attribute to the extra month of prenatal development that I didn't get. For instance, my left foot is a half size longer than the right, and my left nipple is a half inch higher than the right. My wife and kids will tell you that my brain function also is impaired.

*It Started with a Pickle Crock* covers my childhood, from my big sister exploiting and squabbling with me, to ill-advised neighborhood games, to adolescent science experiments, to poker. Ah yes, poker. I move on to football, a big part of my early life, and to dancing, a big worry of my early life, and present-day life for that matter. The prospect of dancing makes me very uneasy, sweat excessively, and think unclearly, even more so than I do already.

Most of my life has been as an adult, at least physically, so I delve into such grownup affairs as customer service battles, irresponsible parenting, vacation mishaps, workplace weirdness, beer, and gruesome animal tales. I take an impartial look at spousal arguments (they're all her fault), and list words and phrases which my family has banned me from saying. I recap injuries I've suffered over a lifetime of activity and, as a budding writer, I present to you some unfinished stories which, if I had more discipline, could become bestsellers. My 8-month-baby mind tells me so.

Footnotes appear throughout the book to explain archaic technology and other things to my millennial readers, if any. Some of you may think that I'm picking on millennials and you're probably right. I have two of them myself, Joel and Matt who I love dearly, but they're worthy of getting picked on. Hell knows they pick on me!

I pride myself on being open and can eschew personal biases. Therefore, I don't blame millennials for ruining the golf, diamond, cereal, and travel industries like some people do, or for the demise of bar soap and napkins, formulating strange baby names, causing poor Olympics ratings, ending the running boom, and killing trees. However, I do blame the white University of Hartford millennial who put clam chowder in her black roommate's hair products and also put the roommate's toothbrush "places where the sun doesn't shine."

The final chapter is a compilation of random things, one-liners if you will. They lack breadth but together are worthy of a chapter which is in Jeopardy format with answers and questions. Ready? Hands on buzzers. Go.

# 1

# *BIG SISTER*

1

My big sister and I pretty much played with our own friends growing up, but we did have our moments together. The first moment I can recall (or have been told) was as a two-year-old in our house on Charles Avenue in Arcata, California. It was a modest two-story house with two towering redwood trees in the front yard. The staircase that connected the second floor to the first was covered in beige carpet and terminated at a landing by the front door.

On that staircase my evil 4-year-old big sister dared me to jump to the landing. I don't recall if they were double-dog dares or just single, but I jumped nonetheless. The jumps became progressively higher until, perhaps four steps up, I landed badly and broke my left foot.

This accident begs the question, where were my parents? Mom was probably cooking dinner and Dad was probably at work, teaching psychology at Humboldt State University.

Mom didn't have a driver's license so she had our cleaning lady, Ms. Jones, drive me to the hospital that night and I remember watching fascinating green lights on the dashboard of her car.

For the next several weeks I was a rambunctious toddler with a foot cast. It didn't slow me down at all as I ate sand in our sandbox, and what I didn't eat I brought back into the house in my cast. Ms. Jones, the cleaning lady, probably wished she'd driven me far, far away instead of to the hospital that fateful night.

2

A random isolated incident? I don't think so. My evil big sister would strike again. This time with intellectual warfare and exploitation. I was a bit older now and still learning the ways of the world with a brain not completely developed in the womb. I craved sweets, conditioned by Mom feeding me cookies as a toddler before bedtime to appease me to sleep, which wasn't widely frowned upon in the '60s. She ultimately appeased my dentist, who would fill my cavity-riddled teeth. So, big sister Wendy knew what to do, sell me candy at a huge price markup.

I received an allowance of 10 cents a week for doing basically nothing. Maybe rinse a dish or two and make my bed. Ten cents a week can add up and Wendy knew that. She made her pitch; a piece of licorice would cost me a dollar. Red or black, the twisted chewy confection was irresistible. Like a drug addict on crack, I just had to have it. And so I did, for a dollar.

Back in the '60s licorice cost a penny per stick, so I could have bought 100 sticks with my dollar at the grocery store. To put the magnitude of Wendy's exploitation (or business savvy) into perspective, 100 sticks of licorice placed end to end would circumnavigate the equator of the Earth $4.12 \times 10^{-7}$ times. Put perhaps a clearer way, 100 sticks of licorice have as many calories as 7.6 Big Macs. Got it? Good.

3

A final incident with my big sister came during the Apollo 11 moon landing. A couple who was friends with my parents was traveling on the west coast and wanted to catch Neil Armstrong's giant leap for mankind. Mom and Dad obliged by offering up our house and, more importantly, our black and white television. Someone actually had to pull a knob to turn on the TV, twist it to adjust the volume, and wrangle the rabbit ears[1] to improve reception. Remote control did not exist and "remote" meant distant, isolated, or inaccessible.

Wendy and I also were fascinated by the historic event, but historic events can take hours to unfold, so we screwed around in the kitchen. Perhaps we were sent there to make popcorn for the adults. At some point we got sidetracked and a conversation happened something like this:

Wendy: "Want it?" (holding out a bag of popcorn kernels)
Bruce: "Okay."
Wendy: "No."
Bruce: "Come on!"
Wendy: "No."
Bruce: "Give me the bag!"
Wendy: "Well . . . alright!"

That's when she slammed the bag over my head, popcorn kernels exploding everywhere with the force of a Saturn V rocket. Kernels in the sink and on the window sill. Kernels on the stovetop and underneath its electric burner coils. Kernels on the kitchen counters and covering the linoleum floor. Kernels.

I believe Dad gave both of us his patented harsh lecture through clenched teeth while firmly grasping the fleshy part of our upper arms. Then we cleaned up the mess the best we could, which turned out to be not very good.

Mom ran the dishwasher the day after the Eagle had landed and our guests had departed. The dishwasher did not cooperate. It discharged sudsy water into the kitchen sink and onto the linoleum floor where a giant puddle began to form. Could it be that the dishwasher's drain line was plugged with popcorn kernels? Yes, according to the plumber's official diagnosis.

The little buggers must have entered via the kitchen sink drain. The plumber went on to say that the dishwasher was toast and a new one would be needed. An encore performance of Dad's patented harsh lecture through clenched teeth while firmly grasping the fleshy part of our upper arms could be expected.

Let's go on to the linoleum floor, shall we? Apparently the infiltration rate of a tiled linoleum floor is quite high. The subflooring became saturated and the linoleum tiles buckled. New flooring would be needed and a third performance from Dad would be forthcoming.

**2**

# ILL-ADVISED NEIGHBORHOOD GAMES

1

Growing up in the Sunny Brae neighborhood of Arcata was fun. A close group of prepubescent boys would assemble after school, on weekends, and on holidays to play. And we played hard . . . and rough. A favorite venue was in the redwood forest on the hills above Sunny Brae. Thickets of pampas grass and bare patches of dirt prevailed in some areas of the hills. We plucked the tall pampas grass with its white feathery flowers to use as spears, and we picked up kiwi-sized dirt clods to use as bullets.

Back and forth we threw the spears and bullets, like the most frenetic cowboy and Indian fight in your favorite western movie. Miraculously no one was ever hurt seriously.

Sure, we sustained some raised welts and bloody cuts, and maybe even shed a couple of tears, but we lived to fight another day.

2

Another venue in the redwood forest we called The Landing. It was a dirt incline about 200 feet long, sloped at perhaps 40 degrees. From trigonometry class everyone remembers that the elevation drop can be written as 200 x sine 40, right? That equals about 128 feet, so going down The Landing was quite the ride. Some rode their stingray bikes with sissy bars[2], some rode go-carts[3], some simply ran, but I preferred to slide . . . on mud.

Looking at precipitation records[4] near Arcata, California, the average annual rainfall is 39.16 inches. In other words it rains a lot in Arcata, which is conducive to sliding on mud. I slid on my butt in knee-patched jeans, never really hurting myself but always getting filthy. I'd bring that filth home to Mom, a filth approaching pigsty status.

I knew the drill, strip down to my underwear at the back door and shiver violently. Then tiptoe through the house in an effort to minimize mud drippings, to the upstairs bathtub. Get a hot sudsy bath going and roll off my frigid taupe underwear. Enter the water and lie back, letting the heat conduct through every joint. After nearly falling asleep and turning into a prune, lather up and clean quickly in the now tepid brown water. Finally, step out of the tub and towel off, leaving behind a crumpled wet towel, a gritty brown tub ring, and the brown water spinning down the drain.

While Mom was slaving away at the washing machine with my muddy clothes, I was comfortably in my pajamas.

She would cook dinner soon, and I would watch a television show, probably something like *Adam-12* or *The Wild Wild West*[5]. Aren't moms great?

3

No-hands football was by far our most ambitious (i.e. stupid) undertaking. "How do you play football with no hands," you ask? Why on bikes riding with no hands, of course. That's right, we actually rode our bikes with no hands on busy Charles Avenue, going out for passes like star receivers Jack Snow of the Rams or Lance Alworth of the Chargers.

We pedaled our stingray bikes with sissy bars hands-free and looked over our shoulders for the flight of the football, which a friend had thrown while pedaling hands-free himself. Sometimes we'd catch it, sometimes we didn't, but we always looked good with Mom's eyeliner penciled below our eyes to replicate the black anti-glare grease of our gridiron heroes. Occasionally we'd get too close to the curb and clip it, catapulting off of our bikes onto someone's front lawn for a relatively soft landing. We didn't score well with the judges though, as flailing arms cost us style points and the botched landing left a huge divot.

# 3

# *ADOLESCENT SCIENCE EXPERIMENTS*

1

As prepubescence gave way to adolescence, my intellectual juices started flowing. I began to wonder how the physical world and natural phenomena worked. In this chapter I aim to entertain as well as educate the reader about natural physical laws. One such physical law is combustion, and as a 12-year-old I learned all about it.

First, the technical definition of combustion; "A high-temperature exothermic redox chemical reaction between a fuel and an oxidant, usually atmospheric oxygen, that produces oxidized, often gaseous products, in a mixture termed as smoke." Okay, now that I got that out of the way we can get on with my story.

Cockroaches have been around since the beginning of time, almost as long as standing in line at the California Department of Motor Vehicles. They are quick, cunning, and nearly indestructible creatures. However, as a 12-year-old I found an innovative way to annihilate them. We were living in tropical Kuala Lumpur, Malaysia for a year where my dad taught during his sabbatical from Humboldt State University. Cockroaches scurried all over our house. Finding Raid too conventional for my taste, I devised the following method to take care of the problem:

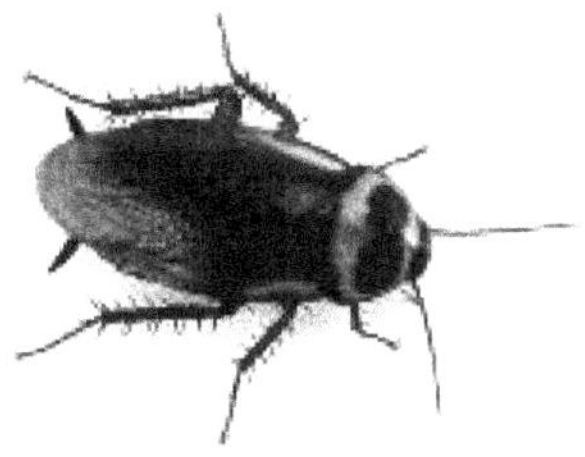

First, hook a spiked leg of a cockroach with toilet paper. Two-ply Charmin worked well but to save money a generic two-ply brand would suffice. Add a few wads of toilet paper into a toilet bowl to form a platform and carefully lower the strand of toilet paper with the dangling cockroach onto the platform. Madagascar cockroaches hiss but the Malaysian cockroaches are much more advanced linguistically; I thought I heard it say, "What the hell are you doing to me?"

Keeping the toilet paper dry is essential as wet toilet paper is not a good fuel (see above combustion definition). Then light the toilet paper with a match, being sure to keep the toilet seat up, not only for the females in the house but also to maintain an adequate oxidant (see above combustion definition).

Flush when the flames are sufficiently high to make you nervous. The resulting smoke cloud is quite satisfying, but knowing that the cockroach is a crispy dead AND is sloshing through the sewer system is a thing of beauty. Burnt and drowned, the NASA-like redundancy of the method is quite impressive.

2

We move on to a dissertation on the ideal gas law; $PV = nRT$ where $P$, $V$, and $T$ are the pressure, volume, and absolute temperature. I had no idea the Swedish distillery made temperature in addition to its popular vodka; many believe that temperature is made by the sun or God. $R$ is the universal gas constant but in my experience gas is quite variable, depending on whether or not I've eaten beans. $n$ is the number of moles of gas which is absurd because everyone knows that gas is made of molecules, not moles.

With the ideal gas law clearly explained let me give an example of its use. As a teenager I was intrigued by fireworks but was always disappointed that they just didn't last very long. If only I could perpetuate a firework. I decided to capture the smoke from a smoke bomb for later use, a reasonable act considering all kinds of things are captured for later use— water in a plastic bottle, creamed corn in a tin can, and pickles in a glass jar for example. A glass pickle jar would be a sturdy vessel, I thought, and I could see inside it as the smoke accumulated.

I closed my second-floor bedroom door and opened a window. No one else was home. I lit the smoke bomb and tossed it inside the pickle jar. I screwed on the lid quickly and set down the jar gently on long red shag carpet.

Soon the jar was engulfed with white smoke . . . and then it happened, an explosion! Let's get back to the ideal gas law, $PV = nRT$. The right side of the equation gets larger after hot smoke particles are released into the pickle jar, so the left side must also get larger to stay equal. The volume of smoke and air does not change (it's just the pickle jar volume), so the pressure must go up and onomatopoeia[6]!

You may be wondering if I was injured. I wasn't, and thank you for your concern. Glass shrapnel littered my bedroom and small fires smoldered in the red shag carpet. Smoke filled the room and started to flow out the open window. I opened the other one. I ran to the bathroom for water and put out the fires. Then I cleaned up the glass pieces and trimmed the burnt strands of shag carpet like a barber.

I took inventory of my bedroom. Besides a few bare patches of carpet the room looked pretty good considering it survived a major explosion and was on fire minutes ago. My parents would never know. When they got home they immediately asked about the smoky smell. I was in big trouble.

3

Our final lesson is on Newton's second law of motion; $F = ma$ where $F$ is the sum of the external forces acting on a body, $m$ is the mass of the body, and $a$ is the acceleration of the body. The body I discuss here does not have arms and legs; it's a shopping cart, and the forces involved are air resistance, rolling resistance, a curb impact force, sliding resistance (friction), gravity, and a hand contact force.

The hand of which I speak was mine or a friends', reaching out a passenger window of Marty's souped-up Ford Mustang to clutch the side of a shopping cart. Marty would gun the Mustang through a mall parking lot late at night and the cart would speed along with us like a motorcycle sidecar until it was released at a top speed of maybe 40 mph.

There's something quite funny about watching a shopping cart speed through an empty mall parking lot. And it's downright hilarious when the cart hits a landscaping curb, somersaults through the air, and tumbles and slides to a gradual stop. It's important to note that the mall was across the street from the Arcata Police Department, and even more important to note that we never were caught.

To summarize the application of Newton's second law: The hand imparted a force on the shopping cart (the mass) which was opposed by the air resistance against the speeding cart and the rolling resistance of the parking lot asphalt against the wheels of the cart. The cart accelerated until the hand released it, at which time it gradually decelerated because of the opposing air resistance and rolling resistance forces, until it smashed against the landscaping curb.

The curb imparted a force which torqued the cart into a somersault. The force of gravity brought the airborne cart back down to the parking lot asphalt where it crashed and eventually slowed to a stop because of friction. That was a mouthful! The primary message from Newton's second law is, of course, the corollary that teenagers in sleepy Arcata obviously have nothing better to do on a summer night than launch a shopping cart. And remember, the next time you struggle to push a shopping cart with wobbly wheels through the aisles of your favorite grocery store, quite possibly some bored teenagers are to blame.

# POKER

1

I remember Dad periodically hosting poker games. I'd inch up to the table and watch grown men drink and smoke, swear and laugh, toss cards and move chips, eat and belch. Looked like a good time to me! And it was, starting with those penny-ante games in Dave Jones' dilapidated travel trailer. Dave Jones, my best friend then and now.

Actually it was his parents' 21-foot Aristocrat trailer, parked in the yard adjacent to their house. The trailer was unkempt and cluttered, but was the perfect place to play poker. It contained a tiny bathroom not fit for the claustrophobic, a loft for sleeping, a fold-out couch, a gas stove, a mini-refrigerator, a well-stocked pantry, a faucet and sink, a free-standing microwave oven, and most importantly a kitchen table with bench seating to deal out the cards. And we had privacy, a cherished commodity for teenagers.

Dave tried to be the perfect host for our first penny-ante game, popping popcorn for us in a pressure cooker prior to our arrival, but he forgot about the oil-filled vessel on the stove in the house. When he finally remembered and removed the lid it exploded, shooting flames up towards the kitchen ceiling.

Not one to panic, Dave coolly ran with the pressure cooker to the bathroom sink to put out the fire . . . the oil fire . . . with water. The flames reached the ceiling this time and singed Dave's face, leaving behind a sooty outline of his body on the bathroom door. He ran outside with the pressure cooker and set it on the ground. Catastrophe averted, but we didn't get our popcorn that night.

2

The gambling bug hit us hard and we gradually progressed to a diverse mix of poker games with larger antes and bet limits. We played 5-Card Draw, Lowball, 7-Card Stud and variants like High Chicago and No Peekum, and many more. But our favorite was a game called Knock.

We could play Knock for hours, sometimes until the sun came up and I rode home on the handlebars of Dave Jones' bike. In Knock everyone starts with two cards. If you think you can win with those cards, or are bluffing, you knock on the table. You win if no one else knocks and then the cards are reshuffled. But if someone else knocks then the high hand wins. Aces are good and pairs are excellent. If no one knocks, then a third card is dealt and play continues as before, then a fourth card if necessary, up to a fifth card.

Here's where Knock got interesting, the loser of a Knock hand would have to pay the amount in the pot for his next ante. The pot could grow quickly and cash reserves could shrink just as quickly. When someone's cash was gone and he owed money everyone at the table laughed heartily at him but, being the sympathetic creatures that we were, we'd offer him the following creative debt reduction options:

**Drink a nasty concoction**. This was Dave Jones' preferred option. The grossness of the drink was directly proportional to the debt. A large debt could require the consumption of a concoction including raw eggs, Tabasco sauce, soy sauce, vegetable oil, curry powder, sauerkraut, anchovies, sour cream, pickles, syrup, and just about anything else we could find in the kitchen. We knew it was a good concoction when Dave's gag reflex kicked in. I was allowed to eat dog biscuits in leu of drinking anything nasty. I found them to be like crackers and not too objectionable.

**Pay the debt over time**. If the debt was large, say a couple hundred dollars, then essentially you were at the mercy of whomever collected the money. He could make you buy him lunch or maybe fill-up his gas tank to whittle down the debt. As the debtor the strategy was to delay these payments until the next poker game when you could go double-or-nothing with the creditor, by each picking a card and the high card winning. Simple and effective, but the debt could balloon even higher . . . until the next poker game when you could go double-or-nothing again.

**Go streaking**[7]. This was a last resort and I recall it happening only once with two people, or four butt cheeks, on the same night. Peter H. and Peter S. had lost a lot of money playing Knock. We talked them into streaking around the block to forgive their debts, although the beer coursing through their systems could have done the talking.

They set out at a good pace, not exactly Olympic-caliber sprinting but certainly grade-school-caliber. Little did they know we were quickly right behind them . . . in a car . . . with the high-beams on . . . and the horn honking. They dashed from bush to bush in the front yards of the houses around the block. Amazingly no one came out of their house with a shotgun at that ungodly time of night. Our car swayed back and forth to keep them illuminated the best we could, but the hysterical laughing was making the car difficult to drive.

The two Peters were, and I have to be careful here so as not to offend anyone, totally exhausted as they completed the circuit and barged back into the house where we played poker. Our diaphragm muscles were quite sore from such excellent comedic entertainment. Thank you to the Arcata residents on Buttermilk Lane, Beverly Drive, Chester Avenue, and Crescent Way for not calling the police that night. They would come-a-callin' on another.

3

My parents were in Europe for a few weeks in the summer of '77, the perfect opportunity to host poker games every night. I was 16 years old and enjoyed the independence and privacy of being home alone, my big sister had already moved into another house with her boyfriend. I'd jog in the morning in the forested hills above Sunny Brae to train for high school football, then drive my sister's AMC Ambassador that she lent me to commute to Denny's in nearby Eureka to wash dishes. When I got home late at night the poker game would begin.

One night a dispute erupted at the poker game and we generated a lot of noise. I don't remember what the dispute was about but I do remember that Greg stuffed my coat down the toilet. The noise didn't subside and soon we had a knock on the door. It was Arcata's finest, a police officer warning us to quiet down. I was mortified but relieved that we only received a wrist slap. The game could continue, in near silence.

I never found out which neighbor complained about the noise, although I suspect it was the Markwells. I hardly ever saw them so we never exchanged glares. Thankfully I didn't have to call a plumber to retrieve my coat from the toilet and my parents never found out about the police visit. But I did have to wash my filthy coat with the other dirty laundry that had accumulated, a chore I seldom did while my parents were gone.

4

Ian was a poker prodigy as a tween. We tried to take his money as greedy teens. It didn't turn out well for us. Ian's parents didn't want him playing poker with older boys, but he'd sneak out of his house to play after we secretly notified him about a game by calling his house and hanging up after one ring, an ingenious code employed by countless teens prior to the invention of the cell phone. Where there's a will there's a way.

Ian consistently won money because he knew when to quit. He'd build up tall stacks of chips and then leave early to sneak back into his house. That infuriated us older boys who'd play into the wee hours of the morning. It was a vicious circle; we'd regularly invite him back to reacquire our money but he'd leave with even more of our hard-earned cash. He was even getting cocky, announcing his accumulated winnings at each poker game.

An investor should always weigh reward versus risk. Ian was no different. The reward of playing poker with us easily outweighed the risk of getting caught by his parents or by mine. My parents left us alone to play at the kitchen table but would occasionally visit the kitchen for a snack. Ian always sat next to the door to the kitchen pantry, a large walk-in room under the very stairs on which I broke my foot jumping as a two-year-old. When Ian heard my parents approaching he'd spring into the back of the pantry, over soda bottles and boxed foods, between shelves of canned goods, and squat down in the darkness. We'd gently close the door behind him. When the coast was clear Ian reemerged from the pantry unscathed, and proceeded to add to his lofty investment returns.

**5**

# *FOOTBALL*

1

Unlike Dave Barry I was good at sports. Eat sh⁸t funny man! I was the number one tennis player at Arcata High School my senior year and earned all-county honors in football. Here's a picture of me in action in front of a packed stadium, and also my 1978 senior yearbook photo showing long hair impinging on my right eye and a classy undershirt framing my thick football neck. Contrast that with no hair and a pencil neck in 2018.

## 2

My football career started with the politically incorrect game of "Smear the Queer," in which everyone tries to tackle the kid with the football. The possessor of the pigskin would dance and juke, often made more difficult by muddy footing, to avoid being tackled. Inevitably the kid would be smothered by a mass of bodies and toss the football aside for the next guy to pick up.

I moved on to organized football in a Pop Warner league at age 10. I played for the fearless, ferocious, intimidating . . . Katnips. That's right, the Katnips spelled with a "K" and not a "C" because we were special (or illiterate). The team name was later changed to the Bobcats for obvious reasons. Our uniforms were blue and white without any hypnotic scent, just the scent of mud, grass, and sweat. We played such teams as the Loggers, Orange Jets, Green Hornets, Yellowjackets, and the Tomcats.

The Tomcats had two players that went on to gridiron glory, Tom Coombs and Willie Beebe. Tom played tight-end for the University of Idaho, my alma mater. One day I was jogging around the track on campus and saw him jogging. I hadn't seen him in over 10 years but somehow recognized his face. His body was totally unrecognizable though, the bulked-up body of a football star. We talked for a few minutes and then went our own ways.

His way took him to the NFL where he played tight-end for two seasons with the New York Jets. Tom's career statistics? One reception for one yard, not exactly stellar but how many of us can say we caught an NFL pass? Willie Beebe was a running back for the University of Colorado and went on to try out for the Denver Broncos but didn't make the team.

That's me (number 55) in the Katnips team picture, with my trusty sidekick Dave Jones to my right and out of uniform. Dave didn't make the minimum weight despite cramming down bananas and water prior to going on the scale, and wasn't allowed to suit-up for the game. If he had made the weight he would have been too bloated to move, let alone run.

I played guard for the Katnips but one game the coach wanted me to try carrying the ball. The rain was falling, typical for Arcata, and the field was muddy. I got the ball and went right but was tackled for no gain . . . by the mud. My feet wanted to move but with each step I sunk deep into the goop and made suction noises. I stumbled, face-planted, slid, and tasted mud. That was my first and last carry of the season.

3

After two years with the Katnips I moved up to . . . the Kittens, another nickname sure to strike fear in our opponents. That's Willie Beebe (number 22) who came from the Tomcats cinching his belt in the Kittens team picture, and me (number 33) not paying attention to the photographer.

In a game on artificial turf at Diablo Valley College in Pleasant Hill, California I literally got the snot knocked out of me. I remember someone on the other team gloating and laughing and pointing at the pooled goo just lying there on the fake turf. I recovered nicely but Dave Jones, who was undoubtedly full of bananas and water to make the minimum weight for the game, wasn't so fortunate. He blew out his knee and was helped off the field. Dave's knee was wrapped in ice and propped up on the back seat of the bus on the long ride back to Arcata. Me . . . I slept on the bus with clear sinuses.

We had another game in Sunnyvale, California. A teammate and I spent the night before the game with our opponent and his family so we could save on lodging costs. The opponent and his older brother felt obligated to keep us entertained so we had a full agenda. First up was the impromptu veering off the road into an orchard. As we bounced along in the family car weaving between some kind of fruit trees, I held on for dear life while the brothers laughed loudly. Where's Child Protective Services when you need them?

Back on the road again we drove to our destination, a remote dirt patch where cock fights were being held. I don't believe the brothers placed any bets but they enjoyed the grisly competition. Boy was this innocent boy from Arcata learning lots! When my family hosted players from the opposing team we simply played ping pong and ate pizza. I got a taste of life in the Silicon Valley, before there was silicon, and the flavor was bad. Give me ping pong and pizza anytime.

4

I had progressed nicely from Katnip to Kitten, and then took the giant leap to become a full-fledged Tiger, the nickname at Arcata High School. My football career had been injury-free thus far, but as a Tiger the injuries started to mount and I knew that I didn't want to play college football.

In a game in Crescent City, California I was poked in the left eye. "How does one get poked through a facemask," you ask? With a finger, a long forceful finger. I saw a white flash and felt a sharp pain. When I couldn't open the eye I decided to head for the sideline rather than play in pirate mode.

The team doctor/trainer told me to get the eye checked out at a local hospital. My parents had driven to the game and were able to take me to a nearby emergency room where the doctor dilated my eye and determined that I had no major damage. I did have floaters, small spots that drifted through my field of vision, and I still do.

We went back to the game which was winding down in the fourth quarter. I remember jogging back to the sideline to be with my teammates, the bright stadium lights blinding my dilated eye. I heard a smattering of applause and the band playing the theme to Rocky[9]. I was embarrassed by the circumstance; here I was, the wounded warrior returning to do battle with that inspirational song resonating throughout the stadium. I didn't do any more battle that night as the game ended minutes later.

I had follow-up appointments with an ophthalmologist back home during which he dilated my eye each time. A student photographer came to my house after one such treatment to take my picture for the athletic awards pages in my high school yearbook. Here's the picture, which appears to show me pissed off and with both eyes dilated. Maybe the ophthalmologist dilated both eyes, maybe the non-dilated eye needed to bug out too, or maybe the photo flash did weird things to my eyes. The point is my look isn't exactly flattering.

5

And then I was concussed. My 8-month-baby brain acted more like a squirrel brain after a vicious hit in another game on a kickoff return. I never saw the guy coming, but most definitely felt his sledgehammer blow.

I didn't hear bells as I fell to the grass, it was more of a buzz. The football came loose and I don't know which team recovered it. I didn't care, I was confused and only cared about getting off the field gracefully. That didn't happen. I stumbled to the sideline and don't remember if the doctor/trainer even checked me out. Mandatory concussion protocol was still decades away and soon I was back in the game, but only physically. Mentally I wasn't all there.

As the defensive captain I called the defensive play by getting hand signals from the defensive coach on the sideline and relaying the play to my teammates in the huddle. My squirrel brain couldn't do it, so I just called the same play over and over again. Soon the game ended and we must have won because the defensive coach never said anything to me about my play calling. Or maybe he chewed me out and I just don't remember. That's football.

# 6

# *DANCING*

1

I love the rain, the pitter-patter of drops, the clean ozone aroma, the flowing gutters and rising puddles. The ambiance sweetens with a breeze to ring chimes and rustle leaves. As a kid I loved the rain too, because rain meant mud and mud meant fun. However, when the rain fell at Jacoby Creek Elementary School I was anxious, particularly if it fell in the afternoon when P.E. class was scheduled. You see, P.E. moved inside when it rained, and we had to dance.

Butterflies filled my stomach when the teacher, Ms. Gorzoch, closed our floor-to-ceiling classroom curtains. My heart pounded when she turned off the fluorescent lights. I trembled when she fired up the record player[10].

I was and still am extremely self-conscious about dancing. I can handle the slow ones, hiding in the arms of a comforting female, but I just know all eyes are on me for the fast ones when my rigid torso and limbs shake awkwardly, like Forrest Gump dancing to *Sweet Home Alabama*.

Unfortunately for me, to get exercise during P.E. we danced predominantly to fast songs. Early '70s hits such as *American Pie, Jeremiah Was a Bullfrog*, and *Roll It on the River* blared through the classroom, which became warm and musty with the gyrations of 30 adolescents. I recovered quickly from the trauma of dancing though, aided by the blast of rejuvenating cool air when Ms. Gorzoch opened the classroom door after P.E. class had ended.

2

Kay was a nice girl. Nice but not especially pretty. An informal campaign to pair me with her infused the eighth-grade social scene at Jacoby Creek Elementary School. I guess the aim of the campaign was to embarrass me, which it did since girls were still pretty icky. I never really talked to Kay, so I'm not sure how she felt about the whole thing. The lead campaigner was Wes Hassler. If ever a surname was appropriate, his was.

Wes also pulled hair, perhaps harder than the rest of us guys did. Most guys had long hair in the early '70s. I know I did. Long hair was a natural target for the probing fingers of adolescent guys with raging hormones. Girls' long hair was strictly off-limits, but guys' hair was fair game and we learned that you could gain full control of someone with a firm grasp of his locks. For most guys the hair pulling was just a phase, but for some the control and power was compelling. They went on to become politicians.

Wes also gave "Melvins," perhaps higher than the rest of us guys did. You know a Melvin (aka Grundy, Gonchy,

Snuggy, Wedgy, Twisty), when a guy's tighty-whities get hiked up to his shoulders, thus flossing his butt crack. If the tighty-whities can be pulled over his head it becomes the infamous "Atomic Melvin" which usually involves ripping.

And that degenerate Wes Hassler executed the dastardly "Jar," perhaps more viciously than the rest of us guys did. The Jar was a brilliant move consisting of grabbing a friend's hand which holds a popsicle and jarring it violently until the popsicle launches.

There's something quite funny about watching a popsicle fly through the air until it splats abruptly on the ground. Jars were executed on Tuesdays and Thursdays, 10-cent[11] popsicle days at Jacoby Creek Elementary School. You could get a Fudgsicle, Creamsicle, Drumstick, and more. Often you wanted more after your first popsicle was melting unceremoniously on the ground.

By the time eighth-grade graduation rolled around at Jacoby Creek Elementary School, the campaign had decided that I would dance with Kay. The graduation ceremony went smoothly, punctuated by our outstanding rendition of *Day by Day*. Then it was time for the graduation dance.

The gym was decorated and we all wore our finest. I sported brown corduroy pants and a tan polyester shirt. Midway through the dance Kay and I met at center court with the other couples. I don't remember how we got there but I suspect we were both nudged. We embraced for a slow dance and it wasn't so icky. I don't remember if we talked or just held on, swaying to the music. Wes Hassler and his cronies had run a successful campaign, and I never saw Kay again after the song ended.

3

Some joker nominated me for Homecoming king my senior year at Arcata High School. I wasn't particularly popular but I was a good student and a good athlete. During the Homecoming football game against Eureka High School, which we lost 15-0, I played fullback and linebacker, and I played with a heavy burden.

My burden was knowing that after the game I would have to be at the Homecoming dance where all the king and queen nominees would be introduced and a king and queen would be selected. I wouldn't be selected and have to dance with the queen in front of everybody, would I? I played okay despite this question running through my head . . . until I couldn't play anymore.

I dislocated my left pinky making a tackle and had to come out of the game. But don't despair, the doctor/trainer popped it back and taped it to my ring finger and I was good to go. I went back in the game with my burden lifted; the doctor/trainer had told me to get my pinky x-rayed after the game.

"After the game" could have meant tomorrow morning, but to me it meant only one thing, I would be at the emergency room getting my pinky x-rayed and would have to miss the Homecoming dance. The x-ray revealed my pinky wasn't broken, and at school on Monday I learned that Wes Hassler, yes that degenerate, was crowned Homecoming king. Actually, Wes was our star halfback and a good guy. He went on to be inducted into the Arcata High Athletic Hall of Fame a few years ago, and I was there to cheer him on.

4

I'm a pretty mellow, relaxed guy. On the morning of my wedding day, for instance, I watched football on television, shirtless and in boxer shorts imprinted with red hearts. I hadn't a care in the world, except for all of my fantasy football players scoring well. But that tranquil disposition disappeared as the time came to leave for the wedding ceremony.

I wasn't worried about taking my vows with Karen, smashing the empty napkin-wrapped wine glass with my foot in the Jewish tradition, or smiling endlessly for a googol of pictures. I was worried about the first dance.

Our guests had arrived and everything was going well until the videographer had me feign running away from my own wedding ceremony and had my groomsmen reign me in. That seemed a bit contrived and juvenile, even for me.

Jean, our Justice of the Peace, botched Karen's maiden name, Sanfilippo, as we took our vows. She had practiced it over and over but at crunch time she pronounced it with an extra syllable, San-fil-ip-pi-o instead of San-fil-ip-po. I think the comic relief may have steadied Karen's nerves, which must have been pretty frayed at the prospect of vowing to spend the rest of her life with me. Jean pronounced us husband and wife, correctly.

We desperately tried to eat some food at the reception but had obligations to well-wishers and the photographer. My facial muscles never wavered in all of our wedding pictures. I actually have decent smiles, but the damn photographer overlooked something very important. See, there I am in an expensive tuxedo with my beautiful bride and her gorgeous bouquet of white roses . . . and my bowtie is crooked for all to see forever[12].

And then it was time for the first dance. I had lobbied for Madonna's *Crazy for You*, but we went with Johnny Mathis' jazz standard *Misty* to please the older family and guests in attendance. Karen and I had practiced dancing slowly to *Misty*, and being in her arms was comforting so I was ready.

I don't remember much about that first dance other than going around and around in circles and deliberately not looking at anyone in the audience. I was focused on Karen's beautiful golden-brown eyes and her smile. Periodically she'd ask me to kiss her, so I'd give her a peck on the cheek or lips. I can't say the crowd went wild, but I suppose they thought it was mildly cute.

One slow dance down and two to go, with my mom and my newly christened mother-in-law, Lee. I got through both of them without any incidents. I did once have an incident in ballroom dancing class at the University of Idaho when the girl I was paired with fell down when we got our feet tangled.

I tried to get off the dance floor after the last note had played for me and Lee, but Karen motioned me back, eliciting some chuckles from the audience. We had more dancing to do, including to some fast songs which induced me into my embarrassing, rigid, Forrest Gump style of dancing. Other couples joined us so I blended in with them the best I could, but as they say, "Oil and water don't mix."

After that the reception was a piece of cake, literally. We cut the wedding cake and, being the man-child that I am, I desperately wanted to smash the cake in Karen's face. But she had warned me beforehand not to and, as a faithful husband, I granted her wish and gently eased the cake into her mouth. I still grant her all of her wishes 30 years later[13].

| 7 |

# *CUSTOMER SERVICE BATTLES*

1

I'm stubborn. My wife and kids will tell you that. When I feel that I've been wronged, I'll fight to make things right. Fight to the end. I've hooked horns with companies such as Sears and Delta Dental, writing letters and emails and speaking with customer service representatives across the globe, with heavy accents and with none at all. Prior to actually speaking with anyone I have, of course, listened to hours of mind-numbing elevator music. I think numbing your mind is part of their strategy so when your moment finally comes to logically unleash your fury you can hardly remember why you're calling.

We bought an AFG 3.1AE elliptical machine from Sears on July 1, 2014, says so right on the receipt which I kept fortunately. Four years later the machine malfunctioned. The resistance was stuck at such a high setting that pedaling just a few revolutions was exhausting, like those final steps a mountain climber takes to summit Everest in the thin air. That's when I called Sears Home Repair and they sent a technician named Logan.

He got on the elliptical machine and tested it out (i.e. Logan's run). Then he cracked open the beast and determined that the problem was a broken flywheel, which was under warranty once I produced the purchase receipt from Sears. He put in the order for a new flywheel and made an appointment to install it the following week. Then he reassembled the elliptical machine so we could continue using it, albeit in Everest mode, until the appointment.

But when Logan reassembled the elliptical machine it was now in centrifuge mode, with all pedaling resistance gone. No big deal since he was coming back the following week to replace the flywheel, or so I thought. This is where the opening bell of my fight with Sears rings, where I add the Sears parts department as a contact to my phone, where my systolic and diastolic blood pressure readings fall outside of the normal 120/80 range.

The Sears parts department was a joke. I called regularly to see if they had ordered the flywheel and every time I was told it was on back order. Two months passed in centrifuge mode, which is not kind to any rubbing body parts. When I told them it had been two months they said they would elevate their effort to get the flywheel and would call me back within 48 hours with an update. I never got a call.

I tried a new tactic. I called the flywheel manufacturer directly and they said they could ship me one in a few days. A few days! That was easy, but I wasn't home-free yet. Not wanting to order (and pay for) the flywheel from the manufacturer since Sears said they would cover the cost under its warranty, I gave the manufacturer's phone number to the Sears parts department. They could get the flywheel in a few days like I was told. They did nothing. I asked to speak to a manager about guaranteeing me that I'd be reimbursed if I ordered the flywheel from the manufacturer. A manager never called back.

So I ordered the flywheel from the manufacturer anyway, got it within a week, and had Logan install it. Our elliptical machine worked great with actual resistance settings between centrifuge and Everest. And I never had to pay the manufacturer for the flywheel once I provided them that purchase receipt from Sears. The moral of the story is, don't rely on Sears to get your parts!

But the story doesn't end there, it only begins. The Sears parts department had UPS deliver me another flywheel a couple weeks later, unaware that Logan had already installed the flywheel that I had ordered. Must have been the infamous flywheel that they had on back order. A large brown UPS van sped up our driveway, taking out some low-hanging pine tree branches and sprinkling dozens of pine cones on the ground, and left the package containing the flywheel on our doorstep. More yardwork for me courtesy of Sears, a cheap parting shot.

What to do with the package? Draw a stick figure of our president on the package (since I can't draw a real figure) and burn it in effigy? Drop the package from the roof of a Sears building? Try to sell the package on Ebay? I decided to be responsible and return the package to the enemy, without any embedded explosives.

I lugged the 25-pound package to our car in 100-degree weather and drove 17 miles to the Sears address on the package with the air conditioner blasting. I parked and forged out into the heat, lugging that damn 25-pound package again. The Sears store was closed. As in out of business. As in the doors were locked and the building was empty. I was mildly surprised because the package supposedly had come from there, but in retrospect I shouldn't have been surprised, with such crappy customer service and competitors like Amazon Prime, going out of business was inevitable.

Annoyed, I left the package by the locked door and drove away. A thought occurred to me a few blocks away, will Sears just resend the package to me? Yes, I concluded, so I drove back and lugged the package yet again into my car and went home.

I figured out my next move, drive to a nearby UPS store and drop off the package. I took my place in line behind a man who was shipping a package. He was chatting nonstop to the UPS clerk who, to my surprise, was actually listening. I wanted to quickly interject that I'd like to leave my package and have it returned to the sender, and then leave, but the man didn't even pause for a breath. How his face didn't turn purple from a lack of oxygen I'll never know.

I had to listen to him brag about the 98 percent Gifted and Talented Education (GATE) score his daughter had and how someday she would be going to Stanford. I couldn't take it anymore and interrupted as he was explaining that his wife was pregnant with another daughter. The clerk told me that she couldn't accept my package and to call the toll-free UPS phone number for a pick-up. A problematic package for me to dispose courtesy of Sears, another cheap parting shot.

When I got home I called that toll-free UPS phone number and the friendly customer service representative told me the package could be picked up the next morning. I told her that I'd leave it by our mailbox on the street (hoping to avoid a repeat of the UPS van speeding up our driveway and taking out more low-hanging pine tree branches).

A brown-shorts-clad UPS man was at our front door within the hour. Caught off-guard on this hot day, I greeted the UPS man half naked. I lifted that damn package a final time and somehow handed it to the man while keeping our dog from attacking him. The package was gone, finally, and my Sears ordeal was over. Over, except for cleaning up a new pile of pine tree debris that the UPS man had left driving up our driveway. A final cheap parting shot from Sears.

2

I have bad teeth. They're clean but are falling apart. The worst teeth are my four bottom molars which have holes that collect food; my own personal food bank if you will. Some dentists have diagnosed the holes as being caused by grinding and have prescribed me a mouth guard to wear at night, or better yet all day. I'm sorry, but I'm not wearing a mouth guard all day. I might have a conversation with someone and they'd struggle to understand my slurred speech, not that I haven't seen confused looks on my listener's faces many times before without any dental protection in my mouth. And the look of a mouth guard isn't exactly classy, with crusty white stains and pockets of drool.

Other dentists have diagnosed the holes as being caused by acid erosion from acid reflux. I'm not aware of heartburn or any other symptoms of acid reflux. I'm only aware of the flux capacitor in *Back to the Future*[14].

I've spent thousands of dollars on the mouth guard, fillings which ultimately fall apart, and in premiums to my dental care provider, Delta Dental. When my new dentist recommended that I get porcelain crowns to protect the holes in my molars, Delta Dental said they wouldn't cover the cost. "Battle stations, battle stations, man your battle stations, this is not a drill!" The following customer service battle with Delta Dental I title, *I Needed Dental Crowns and Got the Royal Treatment.*

Delta Dental told me that the proposed porcelain crown treatment was "to increase vertical dimension and is not a covered benefit." They also indicated that the porcelain crowns are excluded from coverage because the holes in my molars are from acid erosion, not from tooth decay which would be a covered benefit.

At the helm of my weapon, a keyboard, I shot back at Delta Dental explaining why they should pay for the porcelain crowns. I explained that the purpose of the crowns is to protect the holes in my molars, not to change the vertical dimension. I also stated that none of the 22 exclusions in my plan benefit booklet list acid erosion, and that I'm being penalized for having good cleaning habits and no tooth decay, and for having acid reflux which is out of my control.

Then I lobbed a MOAB (Mother of All Bombs), claiming that Delta Dental must maintain another longer list of exclusions to benefits which is not readily available to dental plan enrollees, a clear breach in transparency. "Breach in transparency," buzzwords no company wants to hear.

I wasn't done, I went for sympathy stating that I only want to keep food and bacteria out of the holes in my molars which is a good deterrent to decay and future teeth problems. I asked Delta Dental to reconsider and to contribute towards the long-term well-being of my teeth.

Out of ammo after a barrage of shots, I waited for the surrender. I didn't get one so I appealed to a higher authority, The California Department of Managed Health Care. They saw things my way and convinced Delta Dental to cover the cost of the porcelain crowns. Victory was mine! I had visions of a flag-waving crowd of 200,000 cheering me on as I marched toward the Pentagon with my keyboard raised proudly overhead, waving to my admirers in a blizzard of confetti. A glorious triumph, or so I thought.

I went back to my new dentist for a teeth cleaning, armed with a Delta Dental letter saying that they would indeed pay for the porcelain crowns. Before the cleaning, we had a conversation that went something like this:

Bruce: "When can you do to the crown work?"
Dentist: "I'm not going to do the crown work." Dumbfounded, I pressed on.
Bruce: "Why not?"
Dentist: "I don't feel comfortable doing it." A vague answer. I pressed on.
Bruce: "You were going to do it a few months ago when I was told I had to pay for all of it from my own pocket, why not now?"
Dentist: "I have my reasons." Okay greedy bastard, let's cut to the chase.
Bruce: "Is it a money thing?" He looked me in the eyes.
Dentist: "No."

And then he left the room. I stewed in my juices, wondering what the hell was going on and if I even wanted him to clean my teeth anymore. He returned and opened up a bit:

Dentist: "I'm having personal issues right now so I can't do your crowns. I like you. You're a nice guy. I hope you can understand."
Personal issues? Must be malpractice lawsuits, I thought. Do I really want him to clean my teeth?
Bruce: "Okay, I hope things work out."

He gave me a fist bump which I thought was pretty weird. I wanted my fist to bump his face. And then I had the most awkward and painful teeth cleaning of my life.

I switched to another dentist who examined my teeth and agreed that I needed crowns on my four bottom molars. But because the wear on the molars was so severe, he would only install more durable zirconia crowns. Total cost to me: $2,952. I fought the good fight and lost. But at least I can chew my food now without saving some of it in my molars for a midnight snack.

3

This customer service battle is unique because I was a customer of the California Highway Patrol (CHP). An unwilling customer. One who received a speeding ticket near Clear Lake, the largest natural freshwater lake in California. Karen and I were racing down a hill on two-lane Highway 20 in our 2009 Ford Escape. A stealthy CHP officer was parked in the shade of a tree at the bottom of the hill with his radar gun pointed at us. I saw him just before we whizzed by and took my foot off the accelerator, hoping that he was a nice guy. He wasn't.

His red and blue patrol car lights flashed and he was on my butt in an instant. Now I get anxious for no good reason when the CHP is behind me without lights flashing, so on this occasion I was quite tense. The next stretch of road was windy and it took me a minute to find a safe spot to pull over. My heart beat hard as he approached the Escape.

He was a fairly young guy with a stern face and shades, just like you'd expect. He checked my driver's license and car registration and was satisfied that I wasn't a felon. Then he asked me, "Did you know you were speeding?"

I said, "Yeah, I was probably going too fast."

He asked, "Is there any reason you were speeding today?"

I said, "I picked up speed going down that hill back there." And then I drew a deep breath and said, "And my mom is dying so I'm hurrying home to be with her."

He didn't believe me. If I were him, I wouldn't believe me. The sad truth is I wasn't lying. He pried further, "Where are you going?"

"To Arcata."

"What's wrong with your mom?"

"Lots of things, but the worst is her kidneys are failing."

"How long has she been sick?"

"A long time."

Then he wrote me a ticket. I believe I was going 15 mph over the speed limit but he showed some leniency and wrote the ticket for 10 mph over which had a substantially smaller fine. He warned me not to exceed the posted speed limit and then we were free to go. We drove away to be with my mom, not exceeding the posted speed limit, for a while.

Mom died the next day, but we made it to Arcata in time to care for her. She wasn't particularly coherent, but I hope that she knew we were there with her. I told her some good news, that I had passed my professional engineering exams for which she had seen me study when I was caring for her the last few months.

She slept a lot so Karen and I watched movies. I remember watching *Moneyball*, a great baseball movie about the Oakland Athletics and its general manager Billy Beane, focusing on the team's analytical approach to assemble a competitive team despite having a small budget. I now associate Mom and *Moneyball* like I associate hot dogs and baseball.

My fine for the speeding ticket came in the mail from the Mendocino County Courthouse in Ukiah, California. I knew I was guilty of speeding and probably should have paid it, but people get out of paying tickets all the time so I thought I'd give it a shot.

I wrote a letter to the courthouse explaining two contributing factors to my ticket, the hill and Mom. I concurred that I was speeding and could pay the fine but asked if Mom dying was an extenuating circumstance. I included her death certificate with the letter, dated the day after my ticket. That's right, I stooped so low as to play the death card. Ultimately I didn't have to pay the fine. Thank you Mom.

**8**

# *IRRESPONSIBLE PARENTING*

1

This is a short chapter so Karen and I must have been responsible parents when Joel and Matt were growing up. That and some incidents with the boys I'm too ashamed to include in the chapter. Incidents at an alpine lake and at restaurants come to mind.

As parents a little "tough love" was necessary to discipline the boys, but mostly we tried to encourage and praise them. Occasionally that praise came in the form of "little white lies," which I told each of our sons when they were in the sixth-grade. They had a P.E. requirement to incorporate tumbles and other gymnastic maneuvers into a dance routine. And while my exuberant praise of their performances may have given them confidence, I laughed inwardly at them. Not the worst piece of parenting, but somewhat deceptive and cold nonetheless.

Joel's dance routine was choreographed to Evanescence's *Bring Me to Life.* He and his partner Mike tumbled and rolled, kicked and threw a soccer ball, and basically just frolicked enthusiastically through space. Joel's signature move was the logroll in which the entire body rolls on the ground with the arms extended overhead.

The dance routine was the culmination of a P.E. unit on gymnastics maneuvers. One such maneuver that they practiced was the cartwheel. Joel wasn't the most nimble guy and couldn't do one without the aid of a belt with handles that the teacher grabbed to rotate him. We dubbed it "the belt of shame" and Joel hated it. Who wouldn't.

Matt's dance routine featured swashbuckling to the *Pirates of the Caribbean* theme song. He and his partner Felix, who was taking fencing lessons, tumbled and rolled and fought with wooden swords. Back and forth they went, up and down they jumped, here and there they engaged until Felix stood over Matt with his blade pointed lethally at Matt's neck. Errol Flynn[15] would have been so proud.

2

Sure Karen and I dropped Joel on his head during an exchange when he was a baby, and we let him build a corral full of maimed and dead ants, but perhaps our worst act as parents was when we scared the hell out of Joel and Matt.

Karen and I walked back to our secluded home, in which Joel and Matt were lounging, after attending a neighbor's party. Darkness prevailed without streetlights or a bright moon, and a steady breeze blew. We subtly tapped at the family room window and secretly watched. Matt was on the computer playing *Roller Coaster Tycoon* and hurriedly left the family room to get big brother Joel. When they returned to look out the window we tapped again and they took off for the master bedroom.

We moved on to the deck where Karen inadvertently kicked a wind chime that was set on a plank to keep it from ringing constantly in the windy conditions. It rang now, freaking out the boys who ran towards their bedrooms. We intervened immediately, our parental alarms finally going off, by calling out to them that it was us. They were relieved at our voices, and rightfully furious by our actions.

No ice cream cone that we could serve them would be large enough, and no video game that we could buy them would be fun enough to make up for our indiscretion. I'd like to think that our hugs and kisses and apologies helped. Nonetheless I'm quite ashamed to say that I have no clue what our motive was, other than the gratification of giving our boys the heeby jeebies.

We'll have to take that with us to our graves, and I'll also bring those incidents that I was too ashamed to include in the chapter. Despite these incidents, Joel and Matt have grown up to be fine young men and we couldn't be prouder. So, Child Protective Services, there's no need to come find us.

3

A father and son out for that first driving lesson, a classic slice of Americana and the first step towards that coveted teen milestone of obtaining a driver's license. Matt was ready to take the wheel, so we went out for a drive in our 2002 Honda Accord. We didn't get very far.

We cruised down our driveway and to the end of Meadow Lane, the private road that we shared with seven neighbors. We were about to turn left from Meadow Lane onto a larger road, but Matt had positioned the car in the middle of narrow Meadow Lane. I spoke up, suggesting that next time he be more to the right in case someone coming from the larger road wants to turn onto Meadow Lane. I got backtalk.

This is where the *Kill Bill* siren sound goes off in my head. You know, the sound when Kiddo sees her enemy and vengeance is imminent. Wanting to set the tone straight on this first outing, I said in a firm voice, "Matt, you must listen to what I say. Our safety is at stake."

Matt wasn't totally receptive to my words as he completed the left turn so I yelled, "Pull the car over now!" He was totally receptive to my words this time and pulled the car over . . . into a ditch. We sat there for a moment as the *Kill Bill* siren coursed through my head again, then I yelled, "I meant pull the car over to the side of the road, not into the ditch!"

He said, "But Dad there's no room on the side of the road, I had to go into the ditch." Dammit he was right, and he'd listened to what I said as instructed. Checkmate. Bad parenting on my part, shouting impulsively to make a questionable maneuver like that.

We made it out of the ditch under our own power, and Matt turned out to be a great driver with no accidents and earning the Good Student Discount for us on our auto insurance policy. No accidents, that is, until one day when the front axle of the Accord broke and the right front wheel collapsed, sending Matt off the road. Fortunately he was able to bring the car to a safe stop. More bad parenting on my part, not maintaining the car.

**9**

# VACATION MISHAPS

1

This is by far the longest chapter. I guess I've taken a lot of vacations, and inevitably something goes wrong. Wrong has many levels, from missing a free breakfast in the motel lobby to missing an international flight, from losing a hotel room card key to losing a wallet or purse, and from being bored to being deathly ill. My stories are somewhere in between, and that's just fine with me.

During one summer break from the University of Idaho I visited my friend Eric at Chico State University. He was towing his undrivable Willys Jeep to the San Francisco Bay Area (I think to sell it) and I rode with him to meet up with some other friends who were catching a few San Francisco Giants games.

Ah, the San Francisco Giants. My team. Darrell Evans, Chili Davis, Jeffrey Leonard, I could go on and on with player names from the early '80s. The Giants weren't particularly good back then, but I loved them nonetheless.

And I loved the home of the Giants, Candlestick Park[16]. Notorious for cold and windy games, Candlestick Park could be warm and sunny too. It didn't matter as long as I was in the ballpark with my friends munching on a hot dog and peanuts and drinking a souvenir cup of soda, reading a Giants program.

We were set to leave for the Bay Area in the morning, but since Eric had to be out of the house he was renting by nightfall we had no place to stay. Two college students with little money and no place to stay. We put our heads together, two innovative but naïve college students, and found some free lodging— at the Bidwell Park Golf Course in Chico, California.

We were stealthy and respectful, waiting until dark to set up our sleeping bags just off of one of the greens, not wanting to put any divots into the manicured grass. It was a pleasant summer night and we slept well under the stars, until we didn't.

Water sprayed our exposed faces peeking out of our sleeping bags and we awakened. Strange to have rain this time of year and the sky was clear just hours ago, I thought in a sleepy haze. But wait, that's not rain, that's sprinklers. Run for your lives!

The sprinklers pummeled us from all directions as we scrambled out of our sleeping bags and gathered up our belongings in the pre-dawn darkness. We stumbled as we tried to dress ourselves hurrying to Eric's Willys, and got there soaked and with armfuls of soggy clothes and sleeping bags.

We dried off on the drive to the Bay Area with the heater on full blast. Soon I'd be watching my beloved Giants, so all was well.

## 2

I liked this girl named Karen. She would become my wife even after a disastrous cruise that we took to the Bahamas. But before I describe the cruise, for you romantics out there I describe my courting of Karen.

She and I had a common group of friends mostly from playing coed softball, and saw each other at social events like post-game pizza dinners, beer parties, and Tahoe ski trips. When she hid my Gumby keychain at a friend's house one night, I knew she was flirting with me.

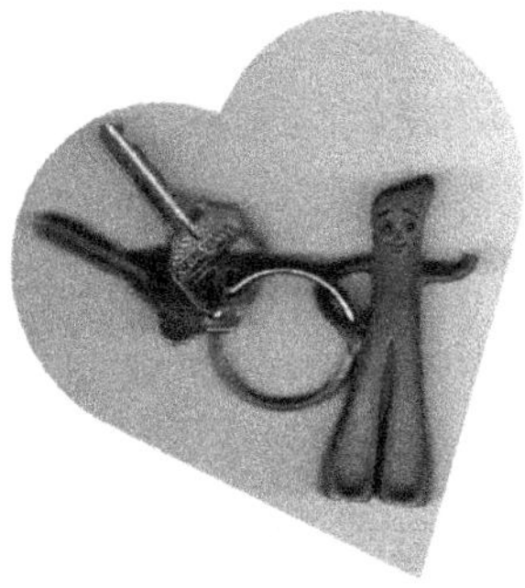

Eventually I asked her over to my condominium and made her dinner. I prepared murtabak, a street food I ate as a kid in Malaysia, which is a square fried crepe filled with minced meat and diced onion and seasoned with curry and other spices. I thought my international culinary sophistication would impress her. If it did, my next move clearly didn't.

I had a VHS tape[17] of Game 6 of the 1986 World Series featuring the New York Mets and the Boston Red Sox. Game 6, when Red Sox first-baseman Bill Buckner had a slow roller go through his wickets to let the Mets win in the bottom of the tenth. Then the Mets went on to win the deciding Game 7 of the World Series. I knew Karen liked the Red Sox and thought we could have a good laugh at the Buckner play.

I was wrong. Badly wrong. So badly wrong that I must blame the indiscretion on my 8-month-baby mind. I brought in the tape, which was set at the Buckner play, and popped it into the VCR[18]. Karen must have thought it was a porno and I was pervert. I hit play and soon she knew I wasn't a pervert; I was an insensitive bastard.

I learned that it's possible to make someone cry on a first date. I know now what I didn't know then; Karen is a die-hard Red Sox fan, ever since she was a teenager to spite her dad, a die-hard New York Yankees fan. The first date ended cordially enough and obviously without any fireworks, and we even went on to have a second date. And that disastrous cruise to the Bahamas.

I'm pretty frugal. Free food is good, a free T-shirt is nice, but a free travel voucher . . . that's practically Nirvana! I got one for attending a timeshare sales presentation. You know, a presentation where the salesman badgers you to buy a timeshare condo and, if successful, celebrates by playing inspirational music like the theme to Rocky[19]. The voucher was good for two people and consisted of a six-hour cruise from Fort Lauderdale to Freeport in the Bahamas, and five days of lodging in Freeport.

So I invited Karen. We flew to Miami in early October 1987 to visit my aunt for the weekend before departing on the cruise to Freeport early Monday morning. Karen had saved her money to buy new clothes for the trip. New clothes that were in her suitcase . . . her missing suitcase.

She vigilantly harassed the airline about her lost bag but by Sunday afternoon she still had nothing— no swimsuit, no snorkeling equipment, not even a change of underwear. Desperate and on a budget, she went to a nearby Kmart and walked the aisles nearly in tears, choosing a few token garments to take to the Bahamas. Luckily the airline delivered her wayward bag late Sunday night, and my aunt could return those wonderful Kmart items and send Karen the refund. We had our glitch for the trip and now the rest would be perfect, right?

A perfect trip would start with a beautiful sunrise on a calm, clear day. Our day was dark, rainy, and windy. We drove from Miami to the port of Fort Lauderdale in our compact rental car. I dropped off Karen with our luggage by the ferry terminal, parked, and then ran back to the terminal through the rain. I entered the terminal looking like a wet cat and saw Karen and a room full of people with befuddled looks on their faces, waiting for a ship that didn't exist.

Seems that our travel voucher was for a cruise ship company that went defunct. Many other young couples, some even on their honeymoon, also had a voucher. We spread like wildfire, seeking all available pay phones[20]. After several panicked and angry phone calls, we collectively found a cruise ship company that would honor our vouchers. However, the ship was leaving in 45 minutes from the port of Miami, which we estimated[21] was at least 45 minutes away.

Time was of the essence. We packed two other couples and their luggage into our compact rental car, and felt we deserved a place in *The Guinness Book of World Records* next to the record for stuffing people into a Volkswagen Bug (18 at the time). The rain was coming down harder now and I couldn't see well out the windshield as we sped away at 70 mph to the port of Miami. We cracked open the windows to aid defrosting the windshield and felt the road spray on our faces.

Somehow we made it just in time to catch the cruise ship. We did have to pay $40 each for a fancy buffet breakfast that was to be served on the ship, but we happily paid and boarded the ship for our six-hour cruise to fun and adventure in the Bahamas.

Once onboard we noticed sanitary napkin bags wedged behind every railing of the ship. That's strange, we thought, and tasteless too, but we were on our way and that's all that really mattered. In retrospect the anomaly should have warned us that something was very amiss, but we ignored it.

Determined to get our money's worth, we overindulged in breakfast as we left the port of Miami. But alas, less than a half hour later those breakfasts were as unstable as the sea. Being highly susceptible to motion sickness even on calm water, Karen was in trouble.

She headed outside to the bow of the ship in a futile attempt to thwart the inevitable, and stood there getting pounded by wind, rain, and spray from the waves crashing against the ship. It was a valiant effort but ultimately she had to hurry back to the door where I was waiting inside and begged me for one of those sanitary napkin bags at which we had scoffed just a short time ago. I gave her a bag and she promptly filled it with her $40 breakfast.

Karen felt better, but the ambiance inside the ship was deteriorating. Virtually all of the sanitary napkin bags were gone from the railings and the ship stank of vomit. Visible puddles of vomit littered the floor throughout the ship. The crew cleaned up as fast as they could, but they couldn't keep up with nearly an entire ship full of very green passengers.

I was one of the few who was unphased by the rough seas and the mass puking. I stayed by Karen's side to offer comfort, and when a man looked around frantically for a sanitary napkin bag and ended up spewing all over his own shoes, I instinctively laughed. Karen told me I should go before she and the other sick passengers mustered up the strength to throw me overboard.

So I went gambling at the casino and ate Seafood Newburg for lunch. Meanwhile Karen lay on a bench with her eyes closed hoping to die, and others moaned and stumbled along and wretched. It was awful, but a glint of hope surfaced when we saw Grand Bahama Island in the distance getting larger. And then it was getting smaller. What was happening?

We later learned that because of Hurricane Floyd, yes that's right HURRICANE FLOYD, the port of Freeport was closed to incoming ships and back in Miami the port had closed just after our departure. We had nowhere to go but out to sea to try to outrun Floyd. Our simple 6-hour cruise now became a 36-hour nightmare.

The crew announced that we would be spending the night on the ship, which didn't have enough rooms to sleep everyone comfortably. I got some Dramamine for Karen that the crew was dispensing like candy. She spent the rest of the night and the next day in a drugged haze, vaguely remembering our overcrowded room and the huge waves rocking our cruise ship as easily as a mom rocking her baby.

We did successfully outrun Hurricane Floyd in the Atlantic and finally reached Freeport the next evening. We were on terra firma, and Karen couldn't be more relieved. The first thing we did when we got to our lame hotel room, which was at least free with the travel voucher, was book a flight back to Miami on Bahamasair rather than cross the Caribbean in another cruise ship.

Our week in the Bahamas was wonderful, except for watching my Giants lose to the St. Louis Cardinals in the

1987 National League Championship Series on television at the tropical bar at our hotel. I drank a strawberry daiquiri in the rain under a palm-thatched roof as the Giants succumbed in Game 7, 6-0.

My crowning achievement in the Bahamas was not killing myself or Karen while driving a scooter to an arts and crafts market. Karen hung on for dear life as I contemplated driving like the British on the left side of the road. Arriving intact at the market, I rewarded myself by purchasing an aqua and white "Yeah Mon" T-shirt.

The beaches were exquisite and I could check out Karen in her blue swimsuit. She didn't disappoint. Just the year before I didn't disappoint her when I stretched on the ground before a softball game in short '80s shorts with legs wide apart.

Our wonderful week in the Bahamas came to an end when we boarded a Bahamasair flight and returned to the mainland without incident. Bahamasair, with its fleet of old propeller planes and uneasy passengers who cross themselves before takeoff.

3

We're national park connoisseurs, having hiked and explored many of them. We collect park brochures and nail park medallions to our hiking sticks. Turns out I wouldn't be doing any hiking, or much walking for that matter, on our trip to Kings Canyon National Park.

The park is beautiful with 14,000-foot mountain peaks, mountain meadows, the swift-flowing South and Middle Forks of the Kings River, and giant sequoia trees. We stayed at the Sentinel Campground and were enjoying the night despite a chill in the air, until a camper drove slowly by our campsite.

I had Joel, who was maybe one year old, bundled in my arms and raced over to the camper to show him its colorful red and yellow exterior lights, like Christmas lights on a Christmas tree. That was a stupid maneuver in the dark on unfamiliar territory and I paid the price when I tripped on a large granite rock.

With Joel in my arms I couldn't touch my hand to the ground to maintain balance like I used to do playing football. Instead, I slammed my left knee to the ground and kept Joel securely cradled in my arms. Slammed it right on a smooth granite rock.

Karen heard us fall and came over to check on us. I was sitting on my butt taking inventory and my knee hurt. I carefully unrolled my sweatpants to see the damage; not too much blood which was good, but the exposed ivory of my kneecap wasn't good.

Joel was fine and not even crying when Karen took him from my arms. She summoned Lee and Charlie, my mother-in-law and her boyfriend, to get the park ranger who was stationed by the campground. The ranger and Charlie helped me walk to the ranger station where the ranger could examine and treat me under lights. The ranger gauzed and bandaged my knee and said I should get more treatment at the nearest hospital in Reedley, California.

Road trip! Over two hours of road trip with my left leg outstretched on the back seat of Charlie's Toyota Corolla. My knee throbbed and felt every bump and turn but we arrived safely at Reedley Community Hospital and took our place in line at the emergency room.

Eventually a nurse took me to a back room into a stall with a bed and a privacy curtain. I waited there for a while and eavesdropped on my neighbor in another stall. A lot was going on, starting with what sounded like projectile vomit. The wreak of alcohol supported my hypothesis. The family was quite angry with the hurler, as if this had happened many times before. The shouting was in Spanish so I didn't understand all the particulars. A nurse took him away to pump out what was left in his stomach and then it was my turn.

Not for stomach pumping, although my stomach wasn't doing so well either with all the nauseating odors coming my way, but for knee stitching. The doctor cleaned and numbed my knee, then sutured me up. Eighteen of them I believe, which formed the letter V. V for Vandals, the nickname of the University of Idaho, my alma mater. Or V for victim, as I was a victim of my own stupidity running in the dark carrying a baby. Or V for vomit so I never forget my hospital neighbor. Or V for vodka, again my hospital neighbor.

I assumed the position for the drive back to our campground, with my left leg outstretched on the back seat of Charlie's Corolla. The numbness in my left knee wore off and the throbbing returned. Charlie and I were exhausted when we reached the campground in the wee hours of the morning. I tried to sleep but that was difficult in a cold tent with a throbbing knee in a sleeping bag on hard ground.

I emerged from the tent after daybreak feeling like a zombie. My research shows that the top ten ways to kill a zombie are:

1. Chainsaw
2. Car
3. Flamethrower
4. Gas explosion
5. Bomb
6. Train
7. Lawnmower
8. Garden tool
9. Baseball bat
10. Firearm

None of these were available except for the car, but the car had no willing driver, so I had to endure the start of a glorious new day in Kings Canyon National Park as a zombie. I walked slowly with an unnatural stiffness the rest of the trip, and grunted after taking any bad steps. Karen kept Joel away from my arms, like any good mother would from the living dead. My appetite was intact, maybe even ravenous, but I refrained from eating any raw brains or guts. My days as a zombie were numbered, and soon we'd be going home.

4

A pretty woman compromised my personal space in Playa del Carmen. Montezuma exacted his revenge in Oaxaca. Karen and Joel had their teeth blackened in Puebla. These are just a few of the mishaps on our two-week odyssey in Mexico in 2006.

Our first stop was in Playa del Carmen, about a 45-minute drive from the Cancun airport, near the northeastern tip of the Yucatan Peninsula. We pulled-up to our hotel in a non-descript gold Chevy rental car, not in the advertised 45 minutes but in a more realistic 1½ hours. We found doubling of driving times to be a good rule given that street and highway signs are placed sparingly, and getting lost was as sure as the next sunrise.

The room in our hotel, the Coco Rio, included a kitchenette and was clean, comfortable, and affordable. We were just off of 5$^{th}$ Avenue, the main thoroughfare where a glut of vendors, shops, and restaurants lined the street, and were only a 5-minute walk to the white-sand beaches of the Caribbean Sea.

Now, if we only had luggage to unpack in our fine room. Without a trunk release lever or a trunk key, our luggage remained trapped in the trunk of the Chevy. I enlisted the help of the hotel proprietor who was bilingual and would be invaluable in explaining my predicament to the rental car agency.

As I sat forlornly in the driver's seat searching for the trunk lever, the proprietor walked out. She was a pretty woman wearing a tube top and short shorts. Soon she began searching for the trunk lever too, leaning into the car and looking under the dashboard in the general vicinity of my . . . umm . . . abdomen. I could only imagine what passersby must have thought, so I skillfully extracted myself from the car.

The proprietor couldn't find the trunk lever either so she got instructions by phone from the rental car agency. They didn't help. A friend of the proprietor was walking down the street so she recruited him to join in the fun. He spoke on the phone with the rental car agency and this time, after some more prodding, he found a trunk button buried deep under the dashboard. We had luggage!

The week in and around Playa del Carmen was wonderful. We saw Mayan ruins in Tulum that were constructed in the 13th century on a striking 80-foot limestone bluff overlooking the Caribbean. For lunch I was appalled to see a Subway sandwich shop at this historic site and protested by eating a taco and drinking from a coconut at a local vendor. Joel and Matt didn't see it that way and wolfed down footlong sandwiches.

We took a ferry over to San Miguel, the only town on the island of Cozumel, and taxied to the pier at the La Ceiba Beach Hotel where we snorkeled the beautiful azure waters. The sunken remains of an airplane and a boat rested there, and a rainbow of colors shimmered from the many tropical fish.

We shunned taking a taxi back to San Miguel and walked the few miles along the waterfront, much to the chagrin of Joel and Matt. You see, the boys had developed a mild case of chaffing the day before rolling in the waves at the beach by our hotel. Sand infiltrated throughout their swimsuits and bodies and walking back to the hotel had reddened their inner thighs. The chaffing was much more than mild now.

The boys strode awkwardly on our trek back to San Miguel. With heads down, feet wide apart, and torsos bent forward at the waist, Joel and Matt waddled pitifully like ducks. The chaffing and our surname of Shaffer led me to christen our family name, "La Familia Chaffer." Toasts at dinner were made to "La Familia Chaffer" the rest of the trip.

We took another ferry to Isla Mujeres where we snorkeled in El Garrafon National Park. We saw more colorful tropical fish in the hurricane-damaged coral reefs and a few rusty anchors. To avoid any further chaffing, we eschewed walking back to the ferry terminal for the return trip and taxied instead.

After a pleasant seafood dinner we were on the ferry back to the Yucatan Peninsula. The ferry had a television which was showing a news story about rioting in Oaxaca, something about striking maestros (teachers) setting up blockades and fighting with police in the zocalo (main square). Riots in Oaxaca, our next destination.

Our flight to Oaxaca went well but not much else did in Oaxaca. After struggling with my Spanish to get the desired insurance coverage on our rental car at the Oaxaca airport, we finally got a white Volkswagen. It even had a visible trunk release lever. If only we had luggage to put in the trunk; Mexicana Airlines had lost it.

Things got worse. A bilingual man in the car rental line overheard me and learned that we were staying at the same hotel as him. He informed us that because of the maestros rioting many businesses in the zocalo were closed, including our hotel. He explained that the hotel moved him to its sister hotel, the Hacienda de la Noria. After a phone call to the Hacienda de la Noria to confirm we were welcome there and a big "thank you" to the helpful man, we were on our way, without luggage, and promptly got lost.

We eventually arrived at the Hacienda de la Noria and collapsed in our room. It was nice enough and the large pool and adjacent restaurant were awesome. Being a few miles from the zocalo, we were in a safe part of town but we would miss out on seeing the wonderful architecture and museums of the zocalo.

That night we watched television in our room waiting for Mexicana Airlines to deliver our luggage. That didn't happen, but we did learn some Spanish by watching English-speaking stations with Spanish subtitles. The boys quickly picked-up on the swear words. We went to bed having only the clothes on our backs and brushed our teeth by chewing peppermint gum.

The next day we drove to the impressive Monte Alban ruins situated on a flattened mountaintop overlooking the Oaxaca Valley. We returned to the hotel and behold, our luggage was stacked inside our room! To celebrate we had a scrumptious chicken molé dinner at the hotel. My next couple of dinners were lighter, however, as Montezuma exacted his revenge on me after I ate a large overripe papaya for breakfast the next morning. Much of this story was originally composed in my head at the head.

We also browsed through ruins in the town of Mitla. Vendors sold their crafts at a market by the ruins. These crafts caught Karen's eye, especially the colorful wood carvings. Her big eyes, open mouth, and appreciative groans did nothing to improve her bargaining position. Soon she was bargaining for porcupine, dragon, gecko, cat, and grasshopper wood carvings. The kind vendor knocked-off a few pesos from the price and everyone was happy.

Our final destination was Puebla, about 80 miles outside of Mexico City. The drive there was hellish with the sun blazing in our faces and an endless string of sharp curves winding through the Sierra Madre Oriental as we crossed the continental divide twice. We paid only one toll, to a small boy. His two compadres held a makeshift rope stretched taut across the road, which they lowered after I paid. The pot-holed road could have used that money for repairs but more likely, I thought, some adults would use it for something else.

Close to 10 exhausting hours later, the last of which was spent fighting downtown traffic, we arrived at our Puebla hotel, the Camino Real. A converted 16th-century convent, the Camino Real was easily the best hotel of our trip. The plant-laden balconies, the stained-glass windows, the large and small courtyards, the beautiful fountains, the ornate décor, and the Spanish architecture were truly wonderful.

We enjoyed the Puebla city center. A bustling street market along Avenue Cinco de Mayo had vendors selling ice cream, candy, balloons, clothing, jewelry, blankets, and more. The zocalo was a beautiful park with more vendors, fountains, and oxidized turquoise copper sculptures. The Biblioteca Palafoxiana held approximately 50,000 priceless books in carved cedar bookshelves that wrapped around a large, high-ceilinged room in three tiers.

Our last dinner of the trip was the most expensive, but certainly not the best. We ate at a Spanish restaurant just down the street from our hotel. Little English was spoken there and even less English was on the menu, so we knew we were in trouble. Matt ordered a virgin strawberry daiquiri and got the sourest margarita that I've ever tasted. I ordered cioppino and thought I was eating the beach as I crunched on sand and small pebbles lodged in the shellfish. Karen and Joel had rice and noodle dishes with a mysterious black sauce. Soon I noticed their tongues, lips, and teeth were black. I had them smile for the camera[22]. We later speculated that the black sauce must have included octopus or squid ink.

The drive from Puebla to Mexico City, where our flight home awaited, took about two hours. Finding the Mexico City International Airport took about one more. You'd think finding a major hub like that would be easy but in the pre-smartphone era it wasn't. We went down a major thorough-fare looking for an exit sign to the airport and saw a small street crowded with vendors where we expected the sign to be. We kept on going and soon were beyond the runways. After turning around, we went down that crowded street and found the airport. We were going home.

Late that night we arrived home and didn't unpack our smelly clothes and souvenirs until morning. We unpacked the colorful Oaxacan wood carvings, beautiful Pueblan ceramics, tasty chocolate, rich molé sauce, and my favorite, kelly-green Mexico World Cup soccer jerseys. We all had a great time in Mexico. All of us, "La Familia Chaffer."

5A

We enjoy river trips. Three whitewater journeys come to mind— a commercial rafting trip down Idaho's Salmon River, and inflatable kayak trips down Arizona's Verde River and Utah's San Juan River.

The Salmon River trip was wonderful with our outfitter preparing meals and setting up our tent by the water each night. A guide navigated our 8-person inflatable raft between the towns of Salmon and Lucile, through several class 2 and 3 rapids, including the Time Zone Rapid where we went back in time from Mountain Daylight Time to Pacific Daylight Time. Periodically the guide put a one-person inflatable kayak, called a duckie, in the river for individuals to try navigating the rapids themselves.

My turn in the duckie finally came. The guide had coached us to paddle around any big rocks, to pick one side or the other. Pretty obvious, right? Before I go any further, let me say that I could paddle essentially using only one arm, having had recent shoulder surgery. I'll now proceed, having firmly laid the foundation for a legitimate excuse.

Many forces in nature are strong— the gravitational force of a massive object, the electric force of a highly-charged body, and the buoyant force of dense seawater, for example. But the attractive force of a boulder in a river is the strongest of them all. As I navigated the rapid, I approached a boulder and calmly told myself to pick one side or the other as I'd been coached. Even the current wanted to take me to one side or the other as the flow split at the boulder. But some river streamlines struck the boulder, churning up water and forcefully pinning any floating debris against the boulder.

I didn't want to be that debris and I panicked as I got close to the boulder. I was powerless to fight the immense attractive boulder force and plowed right into it. No one else had struck a boulder mind you, so I was special. Again, I sense your concern for me so I'm happy to report that I wasn't injured, except for my pride. I paddled frantically and somehow within seconds I pivoted around the boulder and headed downstream to join a raft full of chuckling passengers.

5B

I inadvertently made more people chuckle on our inflatable kayak trip down the Verde River. Each night we prepared a terrific dinner on our propane stove at our campground by the river. Rob, the musician of the group, played guitar while we guzzled post-dinner beers by the fire under the stars.

After a few nights of this enjoyable routine we had generated quite the load of trash. Some of the kayaks had full garbage bags strapped in as we floated back to civilization at our take-out point where we could dispose of the garbage bags. I had one of those kayaks.

I never earned my merit badge for tying knots as a kid in the Cub Scouts. My tenure with the pack was short-lived after a humiliating experience in front of a packed crowd of parents and friends. We were demonstrating our superior upper body strength and I couldn't climb up a rope to touch the ceiling. Disgraced, I left the pack without ever learning the intricacies of tying knots or strapping things in, which brings me back to my kayak story.

We had successfully navigated several class 2 and 3 rapids and were nearing the end of the trip. And then I encountered a "strainer" on one of the rapids, the kayaking term for an overhanging branch. Just as a strainer separates solid matter from a liquid, a willow branch separated me from my kayak as I got too close to the riverbank. I grabbed my overturned kayak, righted it, and eventually hopped back in, but without a merit badge in tying knots the garbage was missing.

Most of our flotilla of kayaks had successfully navigated the rapid and was waiting for me at an eddy. I can only imagine the looks on the faces of my downstream compatriots as flotsam started to appear— my paddle, empty beer cans, torn food packaging, etcetera, etcetera.

They did their best to retrieve the garbage, like hockey goalies snatching a multitude of pucks, but I fear the natural balance of the Verde River was upset that day. I did my best to save face when I floated down to them, but being drenched and garbage-less face-saving wasn't possible. I took the laughs and giggles like a man, but that wasn't enough to earn my merit badge in humiliation. I would have another opportunity to earn it on our inflatable kayak trip down the San Juan River.

5C

Our friend Jack orchestrated the San Juan River trip (as well as the Verde River trip). He knew the river, had all the latest camping gadgets, was a Boy Scout leader versed in emergency preparedness, but mostly was just a fun guy. We paddled through class 2 and 3 rapids from Bluff, Utah (population 320, 2000 census) to Mexican Hat, Utah (population 88, 2000 census) without incident. The incident happened in Mexican Hat after we were off the river.

Named for a curious sombrero-shaped rock outcropping on the northeast edge of town, Mexican Hat had a nice Navajo restaurant for weary travelers like us. More than just weary, I was hurting too. Hurting from a disdain for the portable camping toilet that we used all week along the San Juan River. I shunned using the crapper the last day or two, knowing that a real flush toilet awaited in Mexican Hat. So I quickly ordered some flatbread and other Navajo delicacies and sped off to the latrine.

Being a hygienic guy, I hurriedly placed three pieces of toilet paper on the toilet seat in the restaurant bathroom. Then I took care of some long-overdue business. I sat in that hot, humid stall for a few minutes and began to sweat. After finishing I went to the sink and cleaned up.

I pushed the bathroom door open and approached our table, hearing uncontrollable laughter first from Jack and then from the others. I felt as though I had parted the curtain and was now on stage in the performance of a lifetime. Speech was not possible with such wild laughter, so my friends and beloved wife and sons just pointed. I looked around, thinking perhaps my fly was unzipped. It wasn't.

Then it caught my eye, a flash of wispy white and I knew I had a most disgraceful toilet paper tail. And it was a pretty long one too. Maybe not as long as a monkey's tail but certainly it could have passed for a cat's. Somehow during cleanup I missed a piece of toilet paper, which adhered like glue to my sweaty derriere.

To this day Jack can't visit a public restroom without thinking of me, which I guess is sort of a backhanded compliment. I finally had earned my merit badge in humiliation.

6

We ate a hearty breakfast at the Cliff House in San Francisco overlooking Ocean Beach before going to a rare Giants-Red Sox game. What better way to digest our meals and make room for hot dogs, peanuts, and other delicacies at AT&T Park than to run around on the beach.

Joel ran around on the beach but that wasn't enough, he needed some ballast so he summoned me over to give me a piggyback ride. I'm not one to refuse a piggyback ride, especially from my grown son. I couldn't think of anything diabolical to do while up there to get even with him for the many kelp whippings I'd received on the beach over the years, so I just hung on.

Joel was able to maintain control while running and spinning on the fine sand, and I'm not a particularly small man (175 pounds). And then his gyroscope malfunctioned. For some reason he took a direct route to the Pacific Ocean. I thought about a dismount but that probably would have ended badly. So I put my trust in our eldest son, an intelligent, rational, Valedictorian no less, as we entered the cold Pacific laughing hysterically.

The waves weren't especially large but water is a powerful force, a force that Joel underestimated. He stumbled and then inevitably he collapsed, dropping his all-important cargo. We were soaked and raced ashore to begin the drying process.

That process included emptying our pockets which contained keys, wallets, and phones. The keys were dry with just a few shakes of our hands. The wallets and their contents would require hours of airing out in our hotel room. The phones were toast. Sure, we removed the batteries and dried the phones the best we could. Maybe Uncle Ben[23] could have spared the phones from the scrapheap had we dunked them in his absorbent rice, but saltwater is not forgiving.

Continuing the drying process, I stripped down in our Ford Escape and changed into some dirty sweatpants and my Giants sweatshirt. Then it was Joel's turn to strip down and change. Remember, I couldn't think of anything diabolical to do while riding piggyback on Joel to get even with him for years of kelp whippings I'd received on the beach. I could think of something now. And it was good enough to get even with him for dumping me in the ocean too.

Joel had stripped down and was naked in the car. My car key fob was relatively dry and functioning just fine. I eagerly pressed the red panic button. The car horn blared and attracted a lot of attention, as I had hoped. A horrified look appeared on Joel's face, as I had hoped for even more. As they say, "Revenge is a dish best served cold."

While Joel scrambled to get dressed in the car with the horn still blaring, I stood by the car doubled over in laughter. Soon my family and Joel's best friend visiting from college came over to laugh with me around the car. I eventually showed mercy and silenced the horn. Joel emerged from the car dressed, dry, and totally embarrassed. Mission accomplished. Unfortunately the Giants would lose to the Red Sox that day, but within the week I would have a new phone courtesy of Joel.

7

Maine's a gorgeous state that we've visited a few times. We've stayed at a bed and breakfast in a quaint shipbuilding town at the mouth of the Passagassawakeag River (Belfast), cheered for the Seadogs (Red Sox AA affiliate) at a game in Portland, viewed Stephen King's scary house in Bangor (which has an iron spiderweb front gate), eaten wonderful blueberry products in Bar Harbor, and seen the first light of day in the U.S. on Cadillac Mountain in Acadia National Park.

Our most recent trip to Maine was gorgeous as well, but some unwelcome intruders to our lakeside rental house made it uglier. We met Karen's cousin and her family in Naples on Long Lake in the summer of 2015. They had a motor boat so we could explore Long lake and other water bodies in the area. One day we boated south to Brandy Pond and the Songo

River, and passed through the historic manually-operated Songo Lock on our short journey to Sebago lake.

We also boated on Long Lake in a canoe that came with the rental house. It leaked and had a bailing bucket, showing a lack of maintenance which also was true of the house. Karen and I slept in the "finished" basement which most definitely was not finished. We noted the following:

1. The bathroom door hit the sink, so getting in required advanced yoga positions.

2. The piping for the shower was exposed, and we had to turn the water on and off by reaching up to a valve in the ceiling.

3. After a rainstorm a puddle of water formed on the fireplace hearth and soaked a pile of clean clothes that Karen had placed there.

4. The carpeted floor was sloped.

5. The bedding was insufficient to sleep a family of four, contrary to what we were told.

And on the main house level we noted the following:

1. Orb-weaver spiders everywhere!

Orb-weaver spiders, the unwelcome intruders I alluded to earlier. They're big nasty ugly suckers with a toxic bite that'll give you a red welt. Orb-weavers have been known to induce deadly heart attacks in sleeping people by crawling across their faces, waking them up, and freaking them out.

They hid in the eaves and covered the exterior windows with their spiral wheel-shaped webs. The crafty orb-weavers forged a symbiotic relationship with us when we played cards at night. The light from our card game would attract moths and other bugs to the windows where the orb-weavers were waiting. We'd look out the windows when the cards were being shuffled, and see a violent attack followed by a sudden and tumultuous drop of struggling parties to earth.

One orb-weaver took up residence just above the front door and we'd carefully duck whenever we went through it. But we had a major security breach returning from dinner one night when the orb-weaver dropped from his perch onto our turf. Perhaps someone got too close to his web and the breeze startled him. Regardless, a massive hunt rivaling the search for D.B. Cooper[24] ensued.

Unlike the D.B. Cooper search, our search was successful. We overcame a lack of help from the cousin's uninterested pet dog to find the missing arachnid. The search ended with a firm planting of Karen's foot on the floor. Case closed, except for the cleanup.

Karen had sent a firm message to the other orb-weavers with her thunderous foot stomping. They left us alone the rest of the trip and were happy to entertain us with their lethal nighttime acrobatics by the windows.

8

"When in Rome do as the Romans do." We've all heard the phrase and know that it means when you're living in or visiting a community you should follow the laws and customs of that community. That's exactly what I did driving my family around Sicily in a cobalt blue Fiat 500L.

We picked up the Fiat rental car at the Palermo airport, and I rolled the dice by deciding not to get any car insurance, which would have bumped the cost way up. We sped off to our rental house in Augusta on the east coast of the island. It felt good manually shifting the gears, which I hadn't done in years, and letting in the temperate Mediterranean air through the windows.

Like the ancient Romans who built a network of aqueducts to tame the water, the Sicilians built tunnels, viaducts, and bridges to tame the landscape. We plowed through mountains and over valleys and streams on our drive to Augusta, maintaining the Fiat at high speeds in fifth gear, following the lead-foot aggressive driving custom of the Sicilians. Some cars still raced past us, but we passed our share of cars too.

We enjoyed a few days based in Augusta, including a day trip to Mount Aetna and Taormina. Returning to Augusta at the end of the day, we passed through Catania, the second largest city on Sicily. Catania has a series of roundabouts that I had to navigate to get home. I've told you about my fear of dancing, but I haven't yet told you about my fear of roundabouts.

That's right roundabouts, those chaotic circular roads where anything goes. I go, but usually not where I want. I either go around in circles, not able to weave through traffic to the outside lane to take my exit, or I go out the wrong exit in a panic and must make my way back to the roundabout to do battle again.

Knowing my fear of roundabouts, Karen thought capturing our progress through the roundabouts of Catania would be funny, so she whipped out her phone to film the event from the backseat. I simply wanted to keep going straight through each roundabout and I did, thank you very much, without hitting anyone and getting a hefty auto body repair bill. I found grunting, yelling, and laughing at critical moments relaxing, which improved my control of the steering wheel, brake, accelerator, and blinker. A successful crossing of Catania, and it's all recorded for posterity.

When we sped off back to Palermo to complete our clockwise circumnavigation of the island, our road ended at a closed bridge. A stream had got the best of the Sicilians, but I imagined their road crews would be on it soon to fix the bridge and re-tame the stream.

I was too cheap to pay for international phone coverage so Google Maps wasn't available on our smartphones to figure out a new route. Not to worry, my son Joel navigated us with an actual paper map to another road that kept us on course[25]. On another day he even navigated us in the dark to an excellent remote hilltop restaurant, over steep and narrow roads that rivaled San Francisco's Lombard Street.

Back on course to Palermo, we made a stop in Agrigento to see archeological ruins. I missed the turn to park at the ruins and thought about doing a U-turn to go back and park. I thought, "When in Rome do as the Romans do," which meant follow the lead-foot aggressive driving custom of the Sicilians.

Over the course of our week on Sicily my driving had become progressively more aggressive. Now was my time to shine, to be a true Sicilian driver. I knew my turning radius was too large to make the U-turn, but as a true Sicilian driver I didn't care and went for it anyway. Near the end of the U-turn I rammed the curb pretty hard and came to a stop. Karen yelled the F-bomb from the backseat while Joel and Matt just laughed. I was blocking traffic.

A native Sicilian driver didn't appreciate my maneuver and subsequent blockage. He flipped me off, which in Sicily consists of bending an arm at the elbow and clenching the fist, then grabbing the biceps of that arm with the other hand. And he honked repeatedly. I hurriedly backed-up the car, completed the U-turn, and pulled into the parking area. I knew then that I wasn't a true Sicilian driver, for if I was I would have reciprocated the flip-off.

The damage to the car was surprisingly minor given how hard we hit the curb, just a slice in the right front tire. It wasn't flat when we returned to the car after viewing the archaeological ruins, so we went on to our rental house in Romitello in the hills above Palermo. The house was nice with an exquisite view of Palermo and the Tyrrhenian Sea, but the garbagemen were on strike so stray dogs roamed amongst the pungent trash bags that lined the steep windy street to our house.

The day came to return the Fiat to the rental car agency at the Palermo airport and they never billed me for the tire damage. I had rolled the dice and won.

**10**

# *WORKPLACE WEIRDNESS*

1

My friend Marty (of speeding shopping cart fame) helped me land my first job at Denny's in Eureka, California. He was a busboy there and I became a dishwasher earning $2.50 per hour during the summer before my senior year of high school. That was good money for me, which helped fund my poker habit.

I remember watching a training video on my first day of work, and learned that the Denny's motto was "Quality service along your way, 24 hours a day." After that the honeymoon was over and I got to work.

The work was okay but the 8-hour swing shift was long and I watched the clock when I wasn't swamped with dishes. The highlight of my Denny's career was when I found a quarter in some mashed potatoes that were plastered onto a plate. Think about it, a quarter was 1/10 of my hourly wage, what a score!

I also scored some tip money from the waitresses who ~~felt sorry for me~~ thought I was doing a good job. The job had some fringe benefits too, like stealing pastries and other desserts from the large walk-in refrigerator, and getting meals legitimately for half price.

Yes, the clock could move slowly but Marty was there to speed it up. As a busboy he usually was cleaning tables out with the customers while I was back in the kitchen with the dishwasher. During slow times Marty would come back to the kitchen and talk, and then toss a piece of food at me or someone else. Food fight!

One food fight was so intense that, with yellow mustard all over his face and on his brown Denny's shirt, Marty reminded me of an Oompa Loompa. Obviously he couldn't go back out to be with the customers looking like that, so I came to his aid by washing his shirt in the dishwasher and wringing it out relatively dry. He was good to go, and 15 minutes had come off the clock.

2

Marty also helped me get a sporadic job mowing lawns at an apartment complex in Sunny Brae. He did some maintenance work there and hooked me up with the property manager. I enjoyed riding the mower and cutting the grass but only did it a few times before my big mouth led to a most unceremonious dismissal.

In college my big mouth learned some things to say. During my senior year of high school I wasn't very aggressive in pursuing colleges to attend the next year, so I ended up in my hometown of Arcata at Humboldt State University. I took an economics class and learned all about Social Security; a portion of a worker's wages are put into the Social Security fund and employers match that amount. Then after retiring the worker gets a monetary Social Security benefit.

I was getting paid in cash ("under the table"), but wanted to get the employers share of money going into my Social Security account, so I asked the property manager if he could do that. He asked me to leave and not cut the grass anymore. And I thought a college education was supposed to open up work opportunities.

3

I worked in cubicle world at the Corps of Engineers in Sacramento, California in the hydrology section. Cubicle world, where you can hear your neighbor's most intimate phone conversations, or thank them for blessing you after you sneeze, or smell their afternoon microwave popcorn snack. Sometimes you can smell other not-so-palatable things too. I know my neighbors did.

I came to work one morning and sat down at my computer and started typing away. Soon I heard my neighbors sniffing and asking what that smell was. I immediately knew what that smell was. That smell was skunk from our dog Kip who had encountered one and left me and Karen to clean him up. Apparently I didn't clean up myself very well. Karen had no such complaints from her neighbors at work. Did I go home and change into something less fragrant? I honestly don't remember, but I certainly should have.

4

We celebrated birthdays at the Corps of Engineers too. Karen was a technician in the hydraulic design section and helped put together the 50th birthday party for her boss. She ordered a singing telegram, the "Red Hot Momma," to entertain and embarrass the birthday boy. A crowd of coworkers gathered for cake and the arrival of the "Red Hot Momma."

She showed up in a sexy red dress with her ample bosom spilling out and went for the birthday boy. He was very receptive to the "Red Hot Momma" and thoroughly enjoyed her rendition of "Happy Birthday to You," sung from his lap in a sultry voice reminiscent of Marilyn Monroe singing to JFK[26].

The birthday boy enjoyed it so much that some magic words slipped out of his mouth and presto, the "Red Hot Momma" slipped out of her sexy red dress, which probably shouldn't have happened at the workplace, especially with the birthday boy's spouse present. Underneath were lingerie and two balloons which had been her ample bosom. After some more playful banter, the "Red Hot Momma" left and the spectators finished their cake.

No heads rolled in the aftermath of the birthday bash, although Karen was mortified by what she had ordered and what had happened. The birthday boy's spouse took the proceedings pretty well, at least until she got home and was alone with him. Corps of Engineers upper management didn't produce any memos or emails addressing risqué birthday parties, and a good time was had by all.

5

A few of us engineers were inspecting a levee erosion site on the Sacramento River when I was working for the California Department of Water Resources. Bill announced that he had to go relieve himself, as will happen when deprived of a restroom for a few hours. He wandered off to a shady tree and unzipped. From a distance we heard a shrill scream and swearing. We went to investigate.

We got to the shady tree and there was Bill, visibly shaken and tucking in his shirt. He told us that he had encountered a rattlesnake, i.e. the snake came face to . . . appendage with Bill. The snake's rattle, perfected after millions of years of natural selection, had done a fine job warning Bill, sending him backpedaling in a panic without getting bit. We were all very thankful that we didn't have to treat a wound.

**11**

# *BEER*

1

You might be thinking this chapter contains stories of me spewing projectile vomit onto places vomit shouldn't be. To the contrary, I drink responsibly. Granted, I've felt pretty good after consuming some cervesas, but I've never engaged in the aforementioned spewing, or woken up in a strange place encrusted with last nights' dinner, or woken up with a strange person or any other lifeform. I'm pretty much what you call a square.

However, I do enjoy watching drunk people as much as the next guy. This is where Dave Jones, my best friend since childhood, enters the chapter. Some of you might be asking, "Is Dave Jones alright with being publicly humiliated in your book?" Good question. The answer is an emphatic, "Yes." It only took a trip to Red Lobster where I bribed him with the all-you-can-eat shrimp platter, his weakness. I would have thrown in a bucket of KFC chicken and even my Willie Mc-Covey bobblehead, but our negotiations didn't come to that.

Here's Dave assuming the classic drinker's position. I won't sugar-coat it by saying he's praying to any sort of deity. I'll call it as I see it; Dave Jones is puking into a filthy toilet, and from the looks of it he has spilled. I remind you that Dave let me print these pictures after feeding him that Red Lobster meal.

Here's Dave executing a crisp hand salute, showing me the respect I deserve as the photographer. It's a pretty good salute overall, but his forearm is not at a 45-degree angle to his shoulders (it's closer to 80 degrees), he's showing too much palm, and the tip of his index finger isn't touching the brim of his hat. And he doesn't remember any of it. Again, Dave let me print these pictures.

Finally, here's Dave waving at a poker game with the giddiness of a Price is Right contestant. He must be winning, although he probably doesn't know it. I suspect he's the banker handing out poker chips, wearing an Angels visor like a banker wears a green visor. That's a good thing for the players at the table when someone not fully aware is handing out poker chips. And nice hair. That's all I got on Dave Jones. He let me print the pictures.

2

I once took Joel and Matt on a tour of the Budweiser manufacturing plant in Fairfield, California when they were kids. Irresponsible? I don't think so. They got to see how beer was made, the third most popular drink after water and tea. Besides, we had just come from the nearby Jelly Belly factory and Daddy needed adult beverages to wash away the sweetness.

Daddy was served free beer samples and pretzels. Before you're quick to judge, I shared my pretzels with Joel and Matt, and they were given soda. But the real lesson here, besides me drinking and driving responsibly, is the lesson in savvy marketing. By giving away beer, Budweiser can entice us to buy it and make a huge profit.

Daddy didn't buy any beer that day but he did buy two CDs consisting of those Real Men of Genius ads. You remember those 60-second Bud Light ads on TV and radio; they paid mock tribute to men in overlooked professions or with eccentric traits. Peter Stacker did the humorous yet seriously-spoken commentary and Dave Bickler sang, the lead singer of the band Survivor (known for *Eye of the Tiger*).

Inspired by the ads[27], I present to you two ads that I wrote. Imagine the stern voice of Stacker, and a boisterous Bickler singing the lyrics in parentheses along with backup vocals from a female gospel choir. It doesn't get any better than that.

### Real Men of Genius Ad #1

Bud Light Presents, Real Men of Genius
(Real Men of Genius)
Today we salute you, Mr. Energetic Power Walker
(Mr. Energetic Power Walker)
Headband, Spandex, and free-weights; you're well-equipped to strut your stuff
(Struttin' your stuff)

The rhythmic stride, the intense eyes, and the puffing cheeks; you put the "ooooh" in smooth

(Oh so smooth)

Spit, no problem. Sweat, you bet. And those armpit rings don't exactly sparkle

(rank dank pits)

So crack open an ice-cold Bud Light, oh pounder of the pavement, because your arms may pump like well-oiled pistons, but your look doesn't quite fire on all cylinders

(Mr. Energetic Power Walker)

**Real Men of Genius Ad #2**

Bud Light Presents, Real Men of Genius

(Real Men of Genius)

Today we salute you, Mr. Outhouse Truck Driver

(Mr. Outhouse Truck Driver)

Speeding down the Interstate with a load of stalls, your cargo's as volatile as radioactive waste

(Plutonium 239)

You deftly control the jostling and tipping, for if you didn't, traffic would be crappy

(Oh crap, crap, crap)

Chewing gum, coffee, and No-Doz; you fight sleep so we can peep

(Doin' the wee-wee)

So crack open an ice-cold Bud Light, oh chauffer of shit, because when nature calls, we call on you

(Mr. Outhouse Truck Driver)

3

Showing off my versatility (or lack thereof), consider the following poem:

I peer into my beer
I see icy beer
That light and frothy foam
Which makes me feel at home
The spotless amber tint
That I wish I could mint
Those effervescent bubbles
Mean I'm in for troubles
I think I'll take a drink
I'll drink 'til I can't think
Why do I do this?
Now I've got to piss
I piss by our house
I piss off my spouse
Where do I go from here?
Why hell I'll drink more beer!

**12**

# GRUESOME ANIMAL TALES

1

Living in rural Placer County for over 20 years, my family has had many run-ins with wild animals big and small, ferocious and harmless, bothersome and inconsequential. My family includes our pets, consisting of cats, dogs, goats, sheep, and even a llama briefly. The llama was supposed to protect the goats and sheep from coyote predation, but we lost a sheep under his watch so I built a pen to secure the livestock at night.

We sent the llama to another home, partly for dereliction of duty but mostly because he regularly spit on me at feeding time. Apparently I was too slow with the grain and he let me know about it, hawking up pungent partly-digested grass and delivering it with amazing accuracy to my head. I countered with a spray bottle, spraying his head with water until the bottle was empty. Then I threw the empty bottle at him and yelled some choice four-letter words, entertaining all family members and neighbors within earshot.

2

I like my lamb chops with mint jelly. Not anymore. Not since the night 433 went down. Tagged to the ear of our hefty Suffolk sheep, the number 433 was her trademark label and hers only. She had no name which was kind of sad really, but then sheep typically are elusive and hard to get to know. Our Boer goats had names— Tomas, Murphy, and Kevin. They presented their dehorned heads for petting and you had to call out a name as you stroked them. But the sheep made no such presentations and were assigned only a number.

The goats and sheep roamed our 2-acre pasture grazing on brush, weeds, and grass. I fed them grain at night to entice them into their pen to avoid coyote predation and to reward them for a hard day of work maintaining the pasture. They eagerly sprinted into the pen to gobble up the grain which was spread between three bowls. The ensuing feeding frenzy was fierce. Occasionally I rode bareback on a sheep which had darted in between my legs to get to a bowl. A broncobuster would have cringed at my riding technique, and I quickly ended up on my butt.

But on that night, the night 433 went down, there was no eager sprint to the pen. The goats and sheep seemed distracted but eventually went to poke at their bowls. That's when I noticed a sheep was missing. I went back into our house, strapped on my miner's headlamp, and returned to the pasture in search of the absent ewe.

I hesitantly traipsed in the dark through the pasture with visions of a cougar gnawing on the missing sheep, then turning its attention to me. I briefly searched and came up empty, then retreated back to the house. Karen, who was in bed because she had an early flight in the morning to Washington D.C., hopped out of bed and drove down to the pasture to shine the car headlights. I Immediately spotted a white fuzzy mass illuminated against the green grass.

I walked over to investigate and could see that 433 was dead. The previous night she had been in the midst of the feeding frenzy. Other than coughing a few times, and possibly a small dip in her voracious appetite, she seemed perfectly fine at the feedings. But now she was dead and would have to lie there until daybreak.

I lay in bed that night thinking about how to dispose of her body. I dealt with three previous sheep deaths by conventional means— burial. I suppose technically I completed only 2 ½ burials since the coyotes left maybe ½ of the third sheep. This time, I thought, I need to make things easier on myself. I wouldn't wield a pick and a shovel and do battle with hard ground for hours until a sufficiently-sized hole was dug. I wouldn't piss on the grave for days to discourage critters from exhuming any snacks. I would try a new disposal method—cremation.

We have a wood debris pile that's burned periodically. It's composed of leaves, brush, and branches, and soon it would have a sheep. I got out of bed the next morning and called the Placer County recorded air pollution message to see if weather conditions permitted burning. They did. I checked my residential burn permit to see if it had expired. It had, years ago. I decided to go to our fire department's annual pancake breakfast at a local elementary school and ask them to renew my burn permit.

Breakfast consisted of pancakes, scrambled eggs, hashed browns, ham, and orange juice. I wasn't very hungry knowing what lay ahead, but managed to clean my plate. The ham even went down despite my mind seeing it as mutton. After breakfast I asked a burly fireman if he could renew my burn permit. He explained that he didn't have any burn permits with him, but if I came to the fire station another day he'd give me one. I thanked him and left, knowing I would burn my debris pile that day without a valid permit, like I had done for years.

I tipped our large orange wheelbarrow on its side and pushed 433 in. No problem. The problem was trying to right the wheelbarrow after the mammoth creature was in. After a few attempts I switched tactics. I went to the pull-on-the-hind-legs-with-all-your-might tactic, but could drag her only about 10 feet before becoming exhausted.

I enlisted the help of Matt, my strong teenage son who was taking a weight training class at school. We went back to the wheelbarrow tactic and I pushed 433 in. Matt pulled down hard on the wheelbarrow and eventually it righted. I thanked him and rolled 433 to a wood platform composed of branches which I had prepared in the debris pile.

I tipped 433 onto the platform and covered her with dry juniper branches to conceal my plan from any potential nosey neighbors. I thought two coins should be placed on her eyelids as the ancient Greeks had done, or a eulogy should be given, but I couldn't muster any clever words. I said goodbye to poor 433 and lit the match.

A raging inferno soon materialized, primarily because of those dry juniper branches. I stood upwind in case any undesirable odors were emitted. I scanned the horizon for an angry neighbor holding a hand over their nose. Soon the debris pile was reduced to a smoldering heap except for the sheep which was still ablaze. I was amazed at this phenomenon and speculated that the lanolin in 433's wool was the cause. Like the Energizer Bunny she just kept going and going.

I checked on 433 sporadically throughout the day. By late afternoon she was much smaller but I had a deadline approaching and would have to extinguish her soon. Joel, my other teenage son, was having friends over dressed in tuxedos and formal gowns for picture-taking by our pond prior to going to their Senior Ball.

Unknown to me, Joel was quite worried about my sheep cremation, expecting to see a black sheep carcass smoldering in the pasture as his friends arrived. He called his mom, who was having drinks with her work colleagues at a bar overlooking the Potomac River. The conversation went something like this:

Joel: "Mom, Dad's burning a sheep in the pasture and my friends are coming over for pictures before the ball!"

Karen: "He's burning WHAT?"

Joel: "The dead sheep. He's burning the dead sheep and it stinks."

Karen: "You've got to be kidding me. He's burning the sheep? Good God!"

Joel: "Do something!"

Karen: "Joel, I'm 3,000 miles away. Just exactly what do you want me to do?"

Joel: "Tell him to stop!"

Despite Joel's lack of confidence in me, I didn't want a flaming sheep greeting his friends either, so I extinguished her at 4:00 p.m. and covered what was left with the orange wheelbarrow.

The picture-taking went well as several other parents and I framed the pond and redwood and pine trees behind our exquisitely-dressed children. The chatter of clicking cameras was reminiscent of the chatter you hear at a supermodel's photo shoot. The mischievous child in me secretly wanted the orange wheelbarrow in the background of one picture so I could laugh at the picture years later, knowing the extreme contrast between the handsome youth and the contents under the wheelbarrow. I wondered if marketing executives get a similar chuckle when their advertisements contain subliminal messages, and if movie directors get a chuckle when their shows contain product placements.

The next morning, day two of the disposal, I unveiled the contents beneath the orange wheelbarrow. I expected to gag at the nauseating odor but was pleasantly surprised by no such fate. There before me was a charred wet slab of meat. I knew burning it would be difficult, and I still wasn't going to dig any hole, so that left one other disposal option, chuck it over the fence.

I easily got 433 into the wheelbarrow this time and rolled her to the back fence of the pasture. She was too heavy to heave over the 4-foot wire fence in one piece, so I tipped her onto the ground, got a shovel from our shed, and split her into two more manageable pieces. Over the fence they went, into the thick blackberry bramble along the bank of a small creek. Our property line extends to the centerline of the creek, so technically I didn't dump on my neighbor's property across the fence, not that they ever would have known.

My two-day ordeal was over and 433 was gone. All of her, except for the oily black residue which didn't wash out of the orange wheelbarrow. May 433 rest in peace, or should I say pieces.

3

We feed our cats well with Friskies paté, Purina cat chow, Temptations cat treats, and of course those impromptu deliveries of tuna, cheese, and milk. The cats don't see it that way as they regularly hunt for additional meals.

They're good hunters, even at their advanced ages. I say bravo, for at my advanced age I look for things at which I'm still good. And I have to look hard. The cats consistently acquire an assortment of kills, but are wasteful and rarely devour the entire animal, and sometimes none of it. The animals and animal parts inevitably end up throughout our house.

The cats possess brilliant artistic skills that might surpass their hunting skills. Their canvas is our floor and a well-placed limb or a dazzling splatter of blood would make Picasso proud.

I'd like to elaborate on the animals and animal parts that the cats deposit throughout our house. I use taxonomy, the science of defining groups of biological organisms on the basis of shared characteristics, and giving names to those groups. My biologist wife and son approve. Note that in my classification system animals can be placed in more than one group. Here are the groups, in no particular order:

**The ISIS Group**. I debated on this group name. It's in poor taste but I went with it for shock value. The Islamic State of Iraq and Syria (ISIS) has been in the news for their cowardly beheadings of innocent captives. Thus, the ISIS group consists of headless animals. These animals include birds, rats, mice, voles, and moles.

**The Frisbee Group**. The Frisbee group consists of mummified animals that can attain great distances when discarded outside, like an aerodynamic Frisbee. To reach a mummified state the cats must hide an animal under a couch or rug and let it cure. Animals in this group include bullfrogs and lizards.

**The Frasier Group**. The Frasier group consists of predominantly crane flies which I call Frasiers in honor of television's Dr. Frasier Crane[28]. In addition to crane flies (Frasiers), this group includes common houseflies and "wrong" flies. "Wrong" flies are super large mutant flies that develop from maggots which reside in the carcass of a rat, mouse, vole, or mole that dies behind books in our bookcase (see unlucky animals of the Shawshank group). "Wrong" flies are just wrong, thus the name. Eventually "wrong" flies become lethargic and succumb to starvation and dehydration, or to the omnipresent fly swatter.

**The Shawshank Group**. The Shawshank group consists of animals that survive their cat encounter and are held captive, like Andy Dufresne in one of my favorite movies, *The Shawshank Redemption*[29]. Often these animals obtain their freedom, like Andy Dufresne, when I scoop them into a shoebox and release them outside.

However, some of these animals aren't so lucky and will be classified in the Frisbee group or will support the growth of "wrong" flies in the Frasier group. Animals in the Shawshank group include rats, mice, voles, and moles.

**The F-Bomb Group**. The F-Bomb group consists of animals that require a time-consuming cleanup, which elicits many conjugations of the F-bomb. If children are present, "Cleanup aisle four!" can be exclaimed. This phrase is also exclaimed after a cat barfs. Animals in this group include de-feathered birds and disemboweled or bloody rats, mice, voles, moles, and rabbits.

All animals and animal parts deserve a proper disposal, except for those in the Frisbee group which should be tossed as far as possible. I toss the remains to my killing field, a thick strip of juniper and other vegetation between our cyclone fence and Meadow Lane. I simply underhand the remains like a softball pitcher, with plenty of arc to clear the fence.

My killing field must have over 100 critters or parts thereof. What will the future generation that discovers this grotesque field of bones think? Most likely that a twisted individual lived there. Maybe I should bury a time capsule to explain the bones and include my animal classification system. Then they'll know what kind of individual lived there.

4

We see debris driving down the road every day. It comes in all shapes and sizes and avoiding it tests our reflexes and dexterity. Debris can be the wayward tire tread, the woefully-packed mattress, the discarded trash bag, or the omnipresent roadkill. I'd like to elaborate on the roadkill, and driver techniques to keep a critter from becoming the next tortilla.

Three driver techniques come to mind— the swerve, the hard brake, and the straddle. Swerving to avoid a scampering animal can be dangerous and ineffective. A driver can swerve into oncoming traffic or lose control of the vehicle. And that scampering animal can dash under your repositioned tire and still become the next tortilla. Braking hard can be a successful avoidance maneuver, but you'll leave half of your tires on the road and send that refreshing beverage into the dashboard. And you better hope that the driver on your tail is paying attention. But the straddle, ah yes, the straddle is my animal avoidance maneuver of choice.

The simplicity of the straddle is a beautiful thing. You simply ease your foot off the gas, stay the course, and straddle the darting animal. It's essentially the do-nothing alternative. As an engineer evaluating project alternatives, the do-nothing alternative can be the most cost-effective. As a husband evaluating home maintenance projects, the do-nothing alternative is always wrong.

My success rate at the straddle is probably 50 only percent, which includes straddling inanimate objects like cans, boards, and food. I tend to be unsuccessful when straddling taller animals. Ducks are not real tall but are tall enough to occupy the entire clearance below my car. My saddest moment as a driver was when I straddled a duck couple, perhaps newly-weds, in love and oblivious to being in the middle of the road. The puff of feathers and the involuntary wing flapping that I saw in my rearview mirror was almost too much to bear.

I saw that same puff of feathers and involuntary wing flapping when I straddled some turkeys. Turkeys are tall and I was pretty sure the outcome of my straddle would not be good, but a whole herd of them crossed in front of me and I had no choice. Can't they fly? If I'm a turkey, and many would say I am, and I see a car closing in on me I'm gonna fly.

My unofficial straddle statistics don't support its success. But the straddle undeniably is a viable animal avoidance maneuver, one that I employ whenever necessary.

5

General Dwight D. Eisenhower said to his troops on D-Day, "Your task will not be an easy one. Your enemy is well trained, well equipped, and battle hardened. He will fight savagely." I couldn't agree with him more after an encounter with an elusive, cunning foe. Though having only a fraction of my size and wit, he angered and befuddled me. This worthy adversary wasn't human, and goes by the sinister scientific name, Rattus norvegicus. He's a rat, and this is a rat tale (pun intended).

It started on a crisp December morning as I prepared breakfast for my teenage sons, Joel and Matt, who were getting ready for school. I heard a ruckus in the adjacent family room and peered over to see our chubby female cat, Cassie, in hot pursuit of something. With four cats in our brood I had seen this many times before. We've had bullfrogs, mice, voles, moles, birds, snakes, lizards, rabbits, and even a bat proudly retrieved for us to behold. The bullfrogs are especially nice when found mummified under furniture in the house after months of tanning (see Frisbee group above).

Cassie was chasing the creature around the perimeter of the family room without success, under the computer desk and futon and behind the wood stove, bookcase, and television cabinet. What elusive creature could this be? Surely it couldn't be a mole which is slow and nearly blind and which the cats typically devour easily. Then I joined in the chase and got a glimpse of what appeared to be a rodent with a long tail; it was a rat! We were in uncharted territory trying to capture the rat, so I came back armed with a yardstick, shoebox, and flashlight.

The idea was to poke and prod the rat with the yardstick until he came out from his hiding place. Then either I would get him into the shoebox for later disposal, or Cassie would get him into her teeth for immediate consumption. Neither happened; I was no match for the fleet-footed critter and Cassie just wanted to play with it, casually pawing at it like she did with her toy mice. I did have a moment of eye contact with the rat when he climbed on the back of the television and I thought about trying to bop him with the yardstick, but I have difficulty killing anything larger than an ant.

The family room was in shambles with furniture, pillows, and books strewn to the center of the room in hopes of exposing the varmint. Finally, the rat took refuge in our Nordictrack treadmill and Cassie and I were powerless to do anything except wait.

I gained a new respect for my stealthy opponent. I knew now that he was worthy of a name. I chose Derek, in honor of a contractor I once loathed because he abandoned our fence project until I complained to the Contractors Board. I vowed to fight Derek to the bitter end, win or lose, 'til death do us part. As I contemplated his next move, which I thought would be to eat wires and render our house black, the spirit world intervened.

Now I'm an engineer by trade, a rational man of science, but when the treadmill belt began to move by itself at random intervals with the power OFF I sensed a ghostly presence, a spiritual being. For the briefest moment I exclaimed internally, "I believe!" but science prevailed and I reasoned that Derek was the cause. Was he taunting me or just exercising on a grander scale than his wheel-spinning hamster brethren? Maybe a rat whisperer could delve deep into Derek's mind to explain the treadmill movement, but I certainly couldn't.

All I knew was that this was one strong rat, a descendent of Mighty Mouse[30] perhaps.

All was still until that night when Cassie began the chase again. Deeming her a worthless hunter, and myself too for that matter, I solicited the help of Orion, our sleek athletic male cat. He was asleep on my bed but I scooped him up and brought him into the family room to do battle. I thought he might see or smell Derek and his innate hunting skills would end this standoff. But Orion calmly ambled out of the family room, still half asleep, back towards the bedroom.

I gave up on the hunt and went to bed. It wasn't the night before Christmas, but I can tell you all through the house not a creature was stirring, not even a mouse, or a rat. Days went by without a Derek sighting. The New Year 2009 came and still no rat. A quick check of a Chinese calendar showed that 2009 was the year of the ox, not the rat. Karma was on my side.

The day came when I was making breakfast again for Joel and Matt and I heard that familiar ruckus of a cat in pursuit. It was Cassie, our lame hunter, and one could presume Derek, my rodent nemesis. I suppose Derek could have escaped days earlier through the sliding glass door that we leave cracked open for the cats and this was a different rat. But after a fruitless 30-minute chase resulting in furniture, pillows, and books strewn to the center of the family room and the rat taking refuge in the Nordictrack treadmill, I was convinced it was Derek again.

I wondered how Derek could survive in the house for weeks and speculated that he nourished himself by making secretive excursions to the cat food bowls, then hastily retreating back to his treadmill fortress. This time I was going to get him. I turned on the treadmill to make noise and flush him out into the open. Let me repeat this faulty logic so posterity can learn from my costly mistake. I turned on the treadmill to make noise and flush him out into the open.

The squeal was ear-piercing, like Janet Leigh's shriek in the shower scene in *Psycho*[31]. I approached the treadmill cautiously but saw nothing unusual. I looked on the floor underneath the treadmill belt and shuddered at the sight before me, a severed rat leg. I was still cautious, for a three-limbed Derek still could be quite formidable, and he was liable to fight with a possessed fury now. Then I saw a spot of blood on the belt and noticed a bulge making it rotate unevenly. The Nordictrack had turned Derek into mincemeat. The battle was over. Derek was dead. Cleanup aisle four.

Normally I don't procrastinate, but under an extenuating circumstance like this cleaning up was the last thing I wanted to do. I waited until Karen came home and told her of the mess. Being the predominate user of the treadmill, she "encouraged" me to begin cleaning immediately. I removed the front casing of the treadmill and she peered in with a flashlight. Something caught her eye under the front roller in the glint of the flashlight. I retrieved a pair of tongs to investigate. It was indeed remnants of Derek which I disgustedly removed from the front roller.

The remnants were reminiscent of the sheep remains I once found after it encountered a coyote, bloody, incomplete, and almost indistinguishable. Forensic analysis wouldn't be required to determine the cause of death, which I officially labeled as crushing, pummeling, or for you CSI fans, blunt force trauma. The rest of Derek would have to be removed from the treadmill belt, but that would have to wait until morning.

Morning came and I removed the rear roller of the Nordictrack, which loosened the treadmill belt sufficiently so that I had access to the underside of the belt and could scrape away more Derek remnants with a spatula. My family wouldn't let me clean the spatula and made me throw it away. Then I thoroughly wiped the belt, the platform, and both rollers with a soapy rag. I sprayed the hell out of a can of air freshener to mask the day-old odor emanating from the treadmill, an odor reminiscent of day-old chicken skin in a garbage can on a hot summer day. Finally, I replaced the rear roller and the front casing and was satisfied that the cleanup went well.

My only worry was that the stench would never go away. I recalled the episode of *Mythbusters* where they hermetically sealed a pig carcass in a car for months to see if a thorough cleaning could eliminate the odor after the pig was removed. It couldn't. However, I'm pleased to report that our treadmill rat stench seems to have disappeared. So here's to Derek, my vanquished rat foe, you were a gallant enemy but no match for the Nordictrack mincemeat machine!

**13**

# *SPOUSAL ARGUMENTS*

1

Karen and I have had our spats like all married couples. My parents once had a spat that infuriated my mom so much that she beat my dad with a celery stalk. We've never attacked each other with vegetables, or anything else for that matter, but the decibel level from an argument has climbed to unhealthy levels in our house.

One source of arguments is haircuts. Karen is armed with an electric razor and sharp scissors so I must do as she says when I sit down on a swivel stool to get clipped. First she buzzes my head and beard with the razor. That usually goes quickly since I'm fairly bald, but occasionally I get nipped and jerk violently which leads to a conversation that goes something like this:

Bruce: "Ouch!"

Karen (exasperated): "You have to sit still!"

Bruce: "I felt something. I just reacted!"

Karen: "I didn't cut you!"

Bruce: "So I jerked just for fun?"

Karen: "You overreacted!"

Bruce: "Do you see a red mark?"

Karen: "No!"

Bruce: "Well . . . I felt something!"

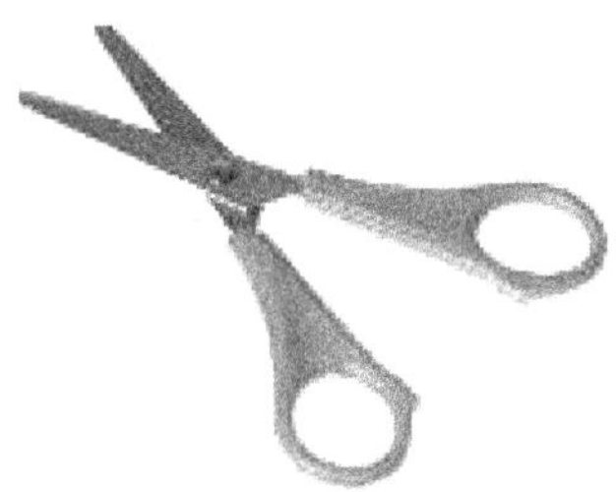

Karen moves on to trimming the uncooperative hairs on my head and beard with the scissors. That involves spinning the stool like a roulette wheel to get just the right angle to cut. When I spin the wheel we lose. When Karen spins the wheel I need a seatbelt to keep strapped in. Back and forth I go like the agitation cycle of a washing machine. The agitation cycle comes to an abrupt end when it's time to cut my moustache.

I pucker and draw my lips together as she carefully trims my moustache with the scissors. Then it's time for the critical cutting of the nostril hairs and a scene from the movie *Chinatown*[32] flashes through my head. The scene involves some thugs slitting private investigator Jake Gittes' (Jack Nicholson's) nose with a knife while he's investigating a murder and mysterious reservoir releases. Thankfully I haven't suffered the same fate as Jake . . . yet.

With trimmed nostrils and no bloodshed, Karen gets to the finishing touches, the back of my neck and my eyebrows. The back of my neck can be a source of nipping and the subsequent arguing as described above. My eyebrows typically go smoothly except for a rogue hair that can get in my eye.

That's it, except when it's time for my summer back shearing. That's right, I have a hairy back but Karen cleans me up like a 4-H sheep going on display at the fair, and she amuses herself in the process. She cuts her initials into my hairy back with the razor and piles the cut hair onto my head. I can shake the pile of hair off my head but must plead with her to erase her initials by finishing the shearing. After sufficient begging she concedes and shears the rest of my back, but then I get a new pile of cut hair on my head.

Now it's time for me to cleanup. My standard of cleaning is, shall we say, a bit lower than Karen's and a new argument ensues.

2

I consider myself a patient guy. As a math tutor I have to be; explaining why 9 times 8 is 72 takes a lot of patience when the tutee doesn't know their times table. I'm patient in everyday life too. I tell Karen that she's too impatient, and she tells me that I'm just slow, which is the crux of many of our arguments.

Take a simple task such as getting into our car and driving away. I usually drive so as we approach the car I'm responsible for pressing the key fob to open the doors. Karen often beats me to the car by the time I grab the key fob from my pocket and push the right button. She repeatedly pulls on the door handle and it clanks at a frequency approaching that of an AM radio station until I open the doors. I get in the car but she doesn't yet.

I live near Sacramento, California where summers can get pretty hot. The interior of the car is an oven and I bake for the few seconds it takes me to close my door, put on my seatbelt, turn on the ignition, and put the car in gear. But Karen refuses to bake and stands outside leaning on her open door, impatiently watching me and shouting instructions to turn on the air conditioner. I take it as a challenge to drive away before she can get in but that hasn't happened yet.

Away we drive with the air conditioner blasting. All is well until we arrive at our destination and disembark. Karen clanks the interior door handle at that AM radio station frequency until I open the doors. We get out and I remind her that I get impatient with her impatience. She reiterates that I'm slow. Discussion over, until our next car ride together.

3

I'm not the best at spatial visualization but I can certainly pack such things as a suitcase, a refrigerator, and a car trunk. I come from good packing stock; my dad drove a cab and was a bellboy when he was young, both of which required packing a car trunk.

While I consider getting all of my clothes into a suitcase a success, Karen considers it a success only if all of her clothes get into the suitcase neatly AND they take up the minimum possible space. Karen excels at packing, coming from good packing stock herself.

Her dad was a Marine and learned that everything has its proper place. In civilian life that meant in his garage every tool was neatly hung on a peg, every box of junk was neatly stored on a shelf or in the rafters, and both cars were perfectly centered. You could eat breakfast off the clean swept concrete floor.

So, I've established that we can both pack, Karen better than me. She subscribes to her dad's philosophy that everything has its proper place. Our arguments arise when we share space in a suitcase or backpack, in the dishwasher or refrigerator, and in the back of our car or SUV. Initially I defended my placement of an item, but now I just remove or abandon the item, walk away disgusted, and let Karen repack it. It's easier that way.

I've tossed clothes on the bed by our open suitcase, set dirty bowls on the counter by the dishwasher, and dropped camping gear on the pavement behind our SUV for Karen to repack. Remember, everything has its proper place and my places are improper. Karen has won this turf war as fierce as any between rivaling drug cartels and, more importantly, I get out of doing work.

4

As I said I usually do the driving, but Karen usually does too, backseat driving from the front seat. To limit her comments on my driving, Karen looks down to read or play games on her phone. We're both happier that way. Sure, I take a wrong turn sometimes but I subscribe to the philosophy that "All who wander are not lost," the slogan on a T-shirt I once wore.

I most definitely was lost in Philadelphia once. I simply went to get our rental car parked two blocks from the restaurant where we had just finished dinner. As I drove the TWO BLOCKS back to the restaurant to pick up my family I somehow ended up on the interstate. I was heading north without a map or smartphone; my only lifeline was a flip phone low on battery.

I pulled over at a gas station in a questionable area and called Karen. We developed a plan to bring me home, almost as daring and difficult as the circumlunar trajectory plan Mission Control developed to bring home the crippled Apollo 13 spacecraft.

I'd head back south on the interstate and announce the exits over my phone as I saw them. Joel would locate those exits on his smartphone and let Karen, who was relaying his information to me on her phone, know when I was approaching the exit I should take. It worked. They reeled me in at the right exit and we reunited after about an hour of wasted time.

So, when I'm driving and Karen's with me in the front seat I think she subconsciously recalls my Philadelphia misadventure and feels obligated to help. Now here's where it gets tricky, sometimes on a road trip I do want her help, but in familiar areas for obvious maneuvers I don't want it.

The latter scenario leads to heated arguments. I admit Karen's caught in a tough spot deciding when to chime in with directions, but does she really need to tell me to make a U-turn when we've reached a dead-end and must turn back? She doesn't have to decide when to give me directions, I'll let her know when I need them . . . which typically is after I've missed a turn. She should have warned me. See, she can't win. There I've vented enough, like that crippled Apollo 13 spacecraft, and they returned home safely to live happily ever after.

5

The distribution of labor in our house is generally me doing the outside work, Karen doing the inside work, and when they were here the kids doing nothing. Arguments arise when chores aren't done correctly or expeditiously.

I'm grateful that Karen does the laundry, the dishes, cooks, cleans, waters the house plants, tends to the garden, puts out the bird feed, shops for groceries, and decorates the Christmas tree.

I hope she's grateful that I maintain the cars, prune the trees and bushes, fix the sprinklers and drip irrigation, clean the gutters, put up the house Christmas lights, burn the debris pile, remove cobwebs and wasps from the eaves, pay the bills, manage the money, do the taxes, solicit repairmen and contractors, change the light bulbs, plunge the toilets, scoop the dog poop, take donations to Goodwill, take out the garbage, clean the water filter, oil the front gate and recharge its battery, unplug the pond outlet, clean the pool, and promote world peace. Sometimes I cook and do the dishes too. I may have skewed the list of chores in my favor.

I used to do the grocery shopping but in a hostile take over bid Karen now does it. She didn't appreciate that I only bought what we needed for the week without getting extras to stock the pantry, so she now stocks it to her heart's content. I only ask that she obey my two maxims of grocery shopping, refrain from unhealthy impulse buys and buy items with the lowest unit prices. Until she can do that I consider her a Shopper-In-Training (ShIT).

The unit price is a beautiful thing when it's posted below the correct item. With the unit price you can be sure you're getting more for your money, the biggest bang for your buck. Of course the biggest bang you get is probably the store brand which may not be the best quality. That's okay with me but not always okay with Karen.

When the unit price isn't posted below the correct item a painful search is required. Or maybe the unit price is posted in esoteric units like $0.26 per count or $0.11 per gram. Sometimes the unit price isn't posted at all and basic math, which is as foreign as calculus to many of us, is needed to compute it. Karen freely admits she'd much rather think about kittens than do any math, so when she shops computing a unit price ain't gonna happen. I'll have to remind her about the calculator on her phone.

A fantasy I have is to equip Karen with an NFL quarterback helmet to wear to the grocery store. I'd send her shopping instructions via the helmet's one-way radio, "Avoid that artery-clogging frosting, cut left at the salami, run to the hummus on sale and grab a few packs." Of course in real life she wouldn't dare wear the helmet, even if it had the logo of the Rams, her favorite team. And not being able to talk back to me over the one-way radio (i.e. swear) would absolutely kill her!

As a ShIT Karen occasionally breaks my two maxims of grocery shopping. We argue about an impulse buy she makes, like a package of chocolate chip cookies. Between bites of chocolate chip cookie I explain to her that I have no willpower and keeping the cookies out of the house is my only chance at maintaining a svelte figure. And sometimes she brings home a national brand like Apple Cinnamon Cheerios with a higher unit price. Between bites of Apple Cinnamon Cheerios I explain to her that Toasted Oats are just fine with me.

Karen argues with me about my propensity to take a long time to finish a job, my job priorities, and if some jobs are even necessary. I argue back that I'm thorough. I concede that pruning all of the trees and bushes on our 4.6 acres took me so long that now it's time to prune them again. Heaven forbid I get hired help! We've been married 30 years and have had a few bumps in the road, but the car just keeps on rollin' merrily along.

**14**

# *BANNED WORDS AND PHRASES*

1

I tend to recirculate previous conversations with my family . . . ad nauseam. My family has had enough, and has banned many of the key words and phrases in these conversations from attaining the audible spectrum. I try my best to accommodate them but slip up occasionally. I present to you the banned words and phrases, in alphabetical order:

**Ball Boy**. Joel once was a ball boy for a Futures tennis tournament, a "minor league" tournament for young tennis professionals. He found the players to be arrogant and rude, constantly yelling at the ball boys and demanding towels to wipe off their sweat. Joel was given a T-shirt for his services which he promptly gave away . . . to me, an avid tennis player.

Consequently, whenever I wear the shirt I say something to him about his ball boy experience. Not anymore, "ball boy" is banned.

**Cabruce**. I was walking behind Karen and Matt when I coined this word. I was the caboose of our short queue and my name is Bruce so . . . cabruce! Pretty ingenious, huh? They thought so too, but after repetitive use while walking behind my family, "cabruce" is now banned.

**Change My Diaper**. I changed my share of diapers when Joel and Matt were babies. If I have the misfortune of needing to wear diapers as an old man it's only fair that Joel and Matt change my diaper. It's the circle of life, if you will. I tell them incessantly that having them change my diaper is on my bucket list. Not anymore, "change my diaper" is banned.

**Chest Bump**. Joel received several academic awards as a high school senior. At the senior awards ceremony Joel's history teacher presented him with a history award, and he did it with flare, launching into Joel with a chest bump, who launched back. I was jealous of their midair antic and vowed to do a chest bump with Joel.

He went away to college so I'd see him just a few times a year, but when I did I tried to greet him with an enthusiastic, sky-high chest bump. Joel would have none of it, until one greeting when he surprised me with a monster chest bump delivered by his 6-foot-2-inch frame. I nearly went down. I still pestered him for more chest bumps after that but he finally reached his saturation point. Mentioning "chest bump" is now banned.

**Clock Tower**. The movie *Parenthood*[33] has a scene where the dad (Steve Martin) envisions his son being a sniper from atop a clock tower after making him play second base in a Little League game, and he commits an error to lose the game. It's a great movie and a great scene, one that I revive whenever I see a clock tower, which happens surprisingly often. Too often for my family, "clock tower" is banned.

**Desserted Island**. If a dessert is on the island in our kitchen I can't refrain from calling it a "desserted island." We eat a lot of desserts. Consequently, my family insists that "desserted island" be banned.

**Neutral Corner**. As we age the tendency for, how shall I say it, passing gas increases. I'm no exception. When the urge comes I announce to my family that I'm going to a neutral corner to rip one, like the boxer who goes to a neutral corner[34] of the ring to let his opponent get up after knocking him down. Obviously I don't knock them down or out with my one-gun salute, but I do annoy them immensely. Did I say passing gas increases with age? "Neutral corner" is banned.

**Nullet**. Maybe I heard this somewhere but I think I made it up. Regardless, I'll certainly take credit for it. Karen and I were visiting Pittsburgh and were at a Pirates game where I saw a man who was mostly bald, with long hair in the back. It was party in the back and nothing up front, a mullet of sorts. Then it hit me, it was a nullet, get it? Karen liked my linguistic discovery but I texted it to the boys and they didn't. I've tried to win their approval repeatedly by reminding them of the word and how it was derived, but they've heard it enough and saying "nullet" is now banned.

2

This concludes the words and phrases that my family has banned me from saying. I'm somewhat proud of those words and phrases, but I've also said some things of which I'm not proud. That usually happens when I spontaneously blurt out something regrettable as an "icebreaker" in a social situation. I don't want my family reminding me of those indiscretions, so I've counter-banned them from saying the following two phrases:

**Just This One**. A park ranger greeted us as we drove up to the entrance of Ronald W. Caspers Wilderness Park in Orange County, California. Pets were not allowed and she asked if we had a dog. I was driving and pointed to the seat behind me where Karen was situated and said, "Just this one." I don't know why I said that, the synapses in my 8-month-baby brain can misfire with strangers, and with non-strangers for that matter.

I laughed but the ranger, Joel and Matt, and Karen didn't. In fact, Karen gave me a death stare which I saw quite clearly in the rearview mirror. The ranger took our entrance fee and we drove away to do some hiking. I've apologized for my verbal diarrhea but nonetheless my family constantly reminds me of that folly, so I've counter-banned them from saying, "Just this one."

**They're an Ugly Bunch**. Karen and Matt dropped me off to play tennis with Claudio, my longtime singles partner. They were going to take a walk while I played and then meet back up with me after I finished. I explained that to Claudio and as they left on their walk I jokingly said to him, "They're an ugly bunch." More synapses misfiring. "The ugly bunch" was just down the street and well within earshot. When they returned my ears received the insults, and to this day they tell the story too often for my liking. "They're an ugly bunch" is counter-banned.

**15**

# *INJURIES*

1

I've had several injuries over the years and my body aches. The primitive stick figure diagram below shows where I've been injured. Why use a stick figure diagram? Because I can't draw, it's that simple. Let me explain.

As an engineer not being able to draw is a setback but one that I overcame to have a successful career. In engineering graphics class in college I scored 100 percent on the first test, one of only two perfect test scores in my college career. After that we did things like construct the third view of an object given the first two views. For instance, below is the front and top views of a relatively simple object. Can you construct the right sideview of the object and draw the actual three-dimensional object?

I certainly couldn't visualize how to do those problems and desperately went to the professor for help. He gave me a lump of clay, which was as effective as a lump of coal, to mold an object and make all of its views magically come into crystal clear focus. They didn't and my grade plummeted to a D, one of only two in my college career (the other was in electric circuits because I didn't study).

Drawing blueprints or anything else for that matter is a problem for me, a big problem. Let me further illustrate my incompetence at drawing (pun intended). Pictionary is supposed to be a fun game, quickly drawing an object and having your partner identify what you've drawn before your opponents, who are doing the same thing, can identify the object. It's essentially charades on paper but it evokes in me the same uneasiness, excessive sweating, and muddled thinking as does dancing.

No one wants to be my partner, so the first order of business is to get me one. After the picker of the proverbial short straw is identified and reluctantly teams up with me, the game begins. I falter as usual and we fall way behind our opponents. Yelling ensues, my partner at me for such lame drawing and me at my partner for looking away from my drawing to see our opponents' drawing since theirs actually resembles something. The game ends when I yell, "I quit!" and walk away.

Satisfied that I can't draw? Take another look at the stick figure diagram below. It may be a bad drawing but it's thorough. With so many injuries I probably should be thankful that I can still walk.

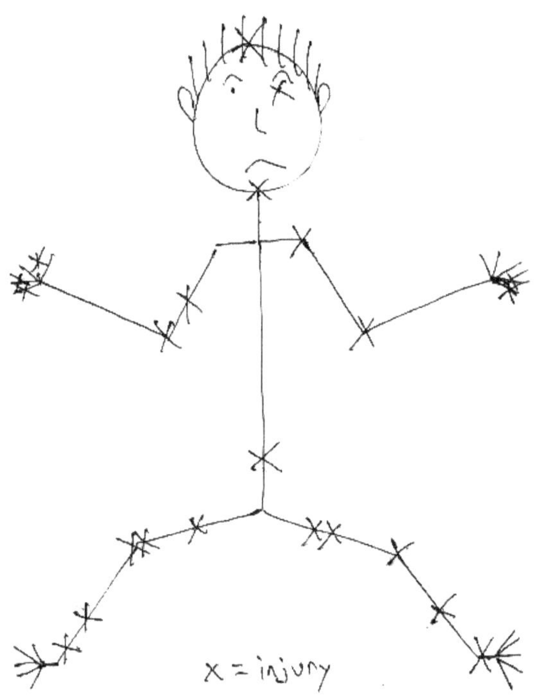

x = injury

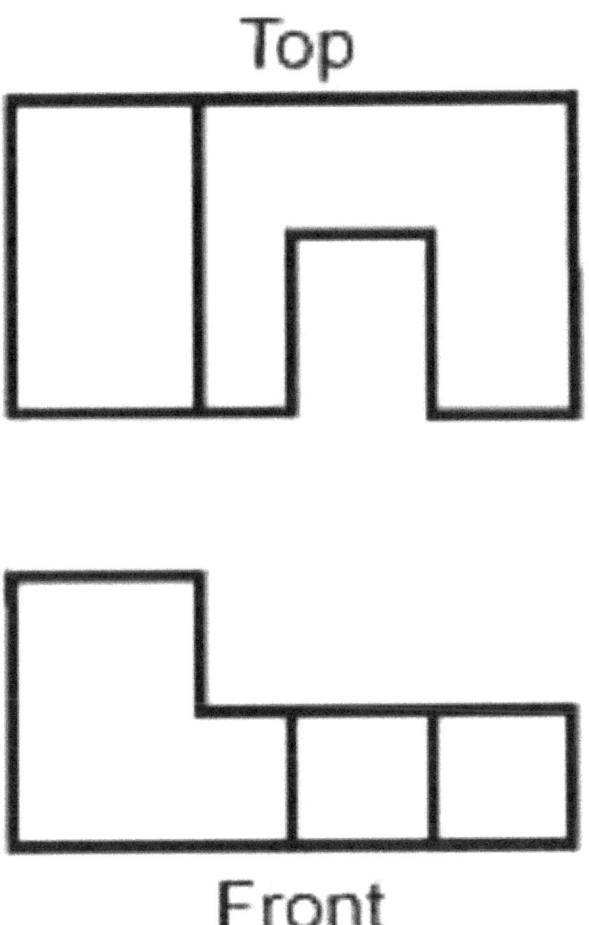


Top
Front

## ANSWER

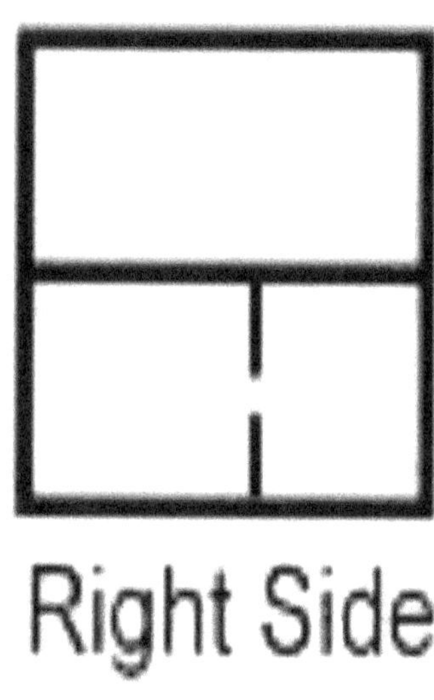



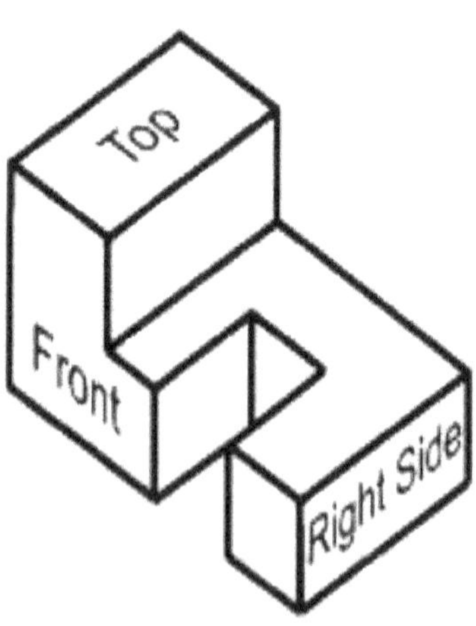

2

Speaking of walking, when I was young I walked like a penguin with my feet pointing way out. That's more of a deformity than an injury but still worthy of discussion. Forrest Gump's momma took him to the doctor for "magic shoes" to straighten out his crooked question-mark back. My momma took me to the shoe salesman for special orthopedic shoes, my "magic shoes," to straighten out my skewed feet. The shoes were shiny black leather with slick souls.

One day when I was six I was shooting baskets on our neighbor's driveway in my "magic shoes." I slipped on those slick souls and fell onto some obsidian rocks (volcanic glass) in the yard next to the driveway. My right wrist struck the obsidian and received a deep gash. It went numb immediately but the sight of the gash scared me and I ran home to Mom bawling.

This time she had her driver's license and took me to the emergency room. The doctor cleaned out the wound and observed two severed finger tendons. He played puppeteer, pulling on the tendons to make sure my fingers could move. They could, and after an operation and several weeks in a cast I could move those fingers on my own.

I probably should have directed my middle finger at the shoe salesman for selling me such slippery shoes, but I didn't know that trick yet. I continued to wear the shoes for a few more years. Below are imprints (pedo-graphs) of my feet dated May 27, 1968 (age seven) that the shoe salesman took to fit me with new shoes. To the untrained eye my feet may appear normal, but to the trained eye of the shoe salesman seeking a commission my feet needed corrections. Today I walk with feet pointed straight ahead, albeit with a limp when my achilles tendinitis flares up.

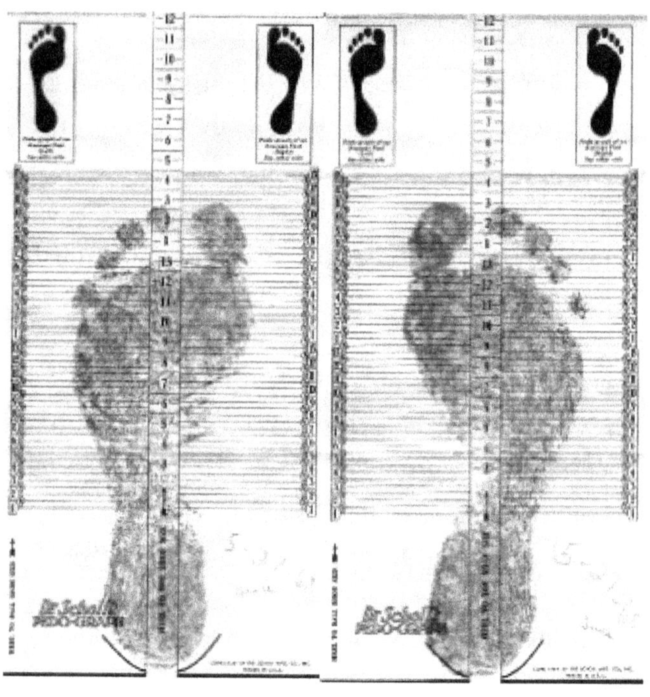

3

I may not be able to draw well but I can sure make fancy tables and graphs. Check out these babies to help you understand just how much my body is messed up. The table is in chronological order of injury and includes details of the injury, how it happened, and how it was remedied, if at all.

The graph has a solid line that shows how I've accumulated injuries up to my current age of 58. The dashed line predicts future injuries over time and appears to show my initials, "BS." It is indeed a "BS" prediction, motivated by a futile attempt to impress you with my graphing skills. Note that the dashed line ends at age 102, which I've determined clairvoyantly to be when I'll die.

| Injury | How Injured | Remedy | Approximate Age Injured |
|---|---|---|---|
| broken left foot | jumping off stairs | cast | 2 |
| severed right hand finger tendons | basketball | surgery | 6 |
| left index finger laceration | cutting frozen hot dog | stitches | 16 |
| poked left eye | organized football | rest | 16 |
| concussion | organized football | rest | 16 |
| left pinky dislocation | organized football | relocation | 17 |
| chin laceration | organized football | none | 17 |
| left elbow dislocation | sandlot football | relocation | 18 |
| right hamstring pull | sandlot football | rest | 19 |
| left quad pull | sandlot football | rest | 20 |
| left hamstring pull | softball | rest | 21 |
| broken right index finger | softball | none | 25 |
| anterior cruciate tear right knee | basketball | reconstructive surgery | 28 |
| left shoulder dislocation | softball | relocation/surgery | 31 |
| medial meniscus tear right knee | softball | surgery | 32 |
| laceration left knee | tripping | stitches | 34 |
| lower back ache | age-related | none | 45 |
| left calf pull | tennis | rest | 49 |
| right calf pull | tennis | rest | 50 |
| right achilles tendonitis | tennis | none | 54 |
| right biceps tear | tennis | none | 54 |
| right elbow tendonitis | tennis | none | 58 |

4

I eats me spinach in quiche, casserole, soup, or just straight-up with butter. I don't chug cans of the leafy vegetable like Popeye the Sailor Man, but I do have something in common with the animated strongman. Take a look at our right biceps. Mine is on the right. We both have an unnatural lump where the normal biceps muscle should be.

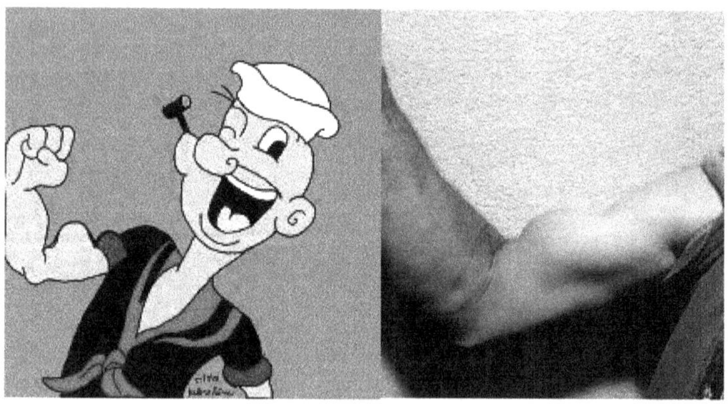

How did I get such a grotesque-looking biceps? Simply look in the nifty table above at the second-to-last entry and see that it happened playing tennis. It actually didn't hurt that badly and I could keep playing. The doctor said my biceps could be surgically repaired but the recuperation time would be lengthy. Maybe I'll do it someday, but for now It doesn't bother me too much except during heavy lifting or repeated twisting, like when I use a can opener for example. So I eats me spinach from a bag instead of a can. I'm Bruce the 8-month-baby man[35].

16

## *UNFINISHED STORIES*

1

Here are two unfinished stories headed directly to the New York Times Best-Seller List when I finish them . . . or not. A warning to all plagiaristic authors, DO NOT expand on my unfinished prose, that most likely would be a complete waste of your time. And my low-budget lawyer would come after you with briefcase blazing. Here's the first potential masterpiece:

*My daughter Yukiko left the hospital room around 8:30 p.m. I hope I was coherent during our few hours together in my post-surgical state, talking about whatever we were talking about. The evening passed by with a hospital volunteer delivering me an all-in-one toothbrush-toothpaste-spittoon assembly, nurses checking in* on me, and a waitperson presenting me with the chef's finest— some sort of blended chicken soup which actually tasted pretty good.

Earlier that day I laid on a gurney in pre-op, going over questions with a nurse. "Why are you here?" he asked.

"To get my left kidney removed."

The nurse looked at his chart and said, "Right," and then made a notation on the chart.

Eventually they let Yukiko in from a waiting room to sit with me in pre-op. I was happy to see her, and she immediately took my mind off of the scalpel that was to plunge into my abdomen soon. We just shot the breeze, and did some math, my old trade when I was a high school teacher. The emblem on the door of the unisex bathroom across from us was a triangle inscribed in a circle.

"What kind of triangle is that?" I asked.

"Equilateral," she said.

"How many degrees is each of its angles?"

"Forty-five ... no wait ... sixty."

"What's the area of the circle, assuming its diameter is two feet?"

"The area of a circle is pi-r-squared so ..." She looked skyward and shortly came back with, "It's just pi!"

"Very good."

Enough math, the doctor was in. My surgeon Dr. Cappitani greeted us and explained the procedure. He would perform a less intrusive laparoscopy to detach my cancerous left kidney and then remove it through a 4-inch incision above my bellybutton.

The cancer had blindsided me, discovered only after some routine blood work revealed a questionable kidney function number, and a follow-up abdominal ultrasound showed a large ugly mass in my left kidney. A week later I'm here, ridding my body of the tumor like I rid my border collie Abe of an engorged tick.

I thanked Dr. Cappitani, a UC Berkely graduate, for explaining the surgery to us, and then he was off. Go Bears! The poor doctor had finished a long surgery involving excessive bleeding. I recalled that I was asked several times if I would accept a blood transfusion if needed. I said, "Yes," and now my answer seemed more plausible than ever.

Dr. Cappitani had a second shorter surgery and then it would be time for mine. I hoped he would eat lunch at some point and wouldn't be hangry and tired during my procedure. I reassured myself that today was probably a piece of cake for him, nothing like the extremely long days of a doctor's residency.

It was time. Yukiko planted a soft kiss on my forehead with a tear in her eye. "Don't worry Cupcake," I whispered, as a relaxant flowing from an IV line subdued my voice, "I'll be fine." Then the masked green-clad surgical team wheeled me away.

My pain level that night after the removal of the kidney wasn't too bad, thanks to an epidural nerve block and generous portions of oxycodone, Tylenol, and whatever else I was given. I didn't feel like reading or watching TV, and just watched people go by in the hallway and dozed in and out. Nurses checked in on me continuously, and other hospital staff came by periodically to prepare the hospital bed next to mine, beyond a giant curtain separating me from who I could only presume would be the great and powerful Oz.

It was just past midnight when they wheeled a man in making lots of gurgling phlegmy noises. He seemed to have lots of discomfort and expressed his suffering by using lots of profanity. Eventually he settled in, and I heard him tell his nurse that he was a veteran. Then he asked her, "Do I have a neighbor?"

I had nothing else to do so I answered him directly. "Yes, I'm Harulo."

"How old are you?"

"Sixty-three."

"I'm Jim, and I'm seventy-four."

"I hear you're a veteran." Then came my chance to thank him for his service, but I didn't for some reason, probably because he didn't pause long enough for me to utter the words.

"Yeah, I served," and that was pretty much the end of our conversation. He clicked on his TV which was showing a ballgame, and then quickly switched over to Fox news. Within minutes Jim was asleep, snoring and making those loud and awful gurgling phlegmy noises, which I later learned were his symptoms of pneumonia.

I wanted to sleep too, but couldn't with all that ruckus next to me. I sprang into action, pushing the call button for my nurse. Soon she came by and since my neighbor was asleep, I asked if she could turn off his TV. In retrospect, what I needed turned off was his labored breathing, and the TV noise was just a minor nuisance. She turned off the TV, and even fetched me earplugs and a blindfold for future noisy and bright TV encounters.

The night wore on. Jim serenaded me through the wee hours of the morning and I knew I wasn't going to get any significant sleep.

*I began playing games with the clock. I'd close my eyes and try to sleep. When they opened up again, I'd note how much time had elapsed. Five minutes was disappointing, 15 minutes was pretty good, and anything over 15 minutes was cause for celebration; a big chunk of elapsed time meant I was that much closer to a hospital discharge.*

*Then a nurse came in to treat me. Time for the ol' catheter removal. First, she measured my urine output, which filled a container 3/4 full. Then she pulled the tube out; ouch, but not as bad as an un-anaesthetized colonoscopy.*

*Two other nurses came in for Jim. His urine output without a catheter was nothing compared to mine. I felt a sense of great pride. With lots of fluid in his lungs and lots of urine in his bladder, the nurses explained that he needed to rid his body of liquid and would have to get up and pee into a container. If he didn't, then a catheter like the one I'd just vanquished would have to be inserted. To me it seemed like a case of dueling catheters, and the iconic banjo tune coursed through my head.*

*The threat of the catheter is powerful; Jim succumbed to the nurses' wishes to get up and pee into a container. I sensed that he was a big man and, being weak from pneumonia, the honorable nurses helped him get out of bed, steadied him, and held the container under his . . . you know. They even shouted accolades as his pee flowed freely; the floodgates had opened.*

*After that I had a few visitors. A nurse came in and gave me a heparin shot in my stomach, which was shaved and fish belly white. Another nurse drew a blood sample from my arm. Yet a third* nurse alerted me to pee into a container, on my own now without a catheter, when the time was right.

The time became right. My nurse unplugged me from the IV that was secured to the back of my hand with a white mesh glove. I would have felt more like Michael Jackson had the glove been covered with sequins.

I walked slowly over to the bathroom with a container in hand, past Jim who I confirmed was indeed a big man. The back of my hospital gown was open and I mooned him, a small consolation for keeping me up all night. I returned to my bed with a half-full container of pee (a pessimist would say half-empty).

My nurse seemed satisfied with the pee output and I eased back into bed. Soon an ultrasound technician was lubing my shaved white fish belly and checking for residual urine in my bladder. The numbers she read out loud were quite small and, according to my hydraulic calculations, my bladder was empty. Great news, I emptied my bladder on my own and was one step closer to being discharged. A bowel movement would have to wait.

Where was Dr. Cappatani? Would he give me the okay to leave?

Breakfast came and I was only able to pick at the hot cheesy omelet and a few grapes. The bran muffin, cereal, and juice would come home with me to help justify the huge medical bill that I would pay.

Yukiko arrived with shake onigiri, rice balls with salted salmon, and planted another soft kiss on my forehead.

"How are you feeling, Dad?" she asked.

"Not too bad. Drugs are a wonderful thing, but the onigiri will have to wait."

"How'd you sleep last night?"

"Well . . . that's a different story. Shoulda got a drug for that."

"Do you know when you can go home?"

"I'm still awaiting word from Dr. Cappatani. I'm surprised he hasn't come by yet. I need to get outta this place."

"We'll go soon enough."

"I hope so. I showed 'em I can pee, let me show 'em I can walk too. Then maybe they'll let me check out."

I rose slowly to my feet and held hands with Yukiko walking through the crowded hospital hallway. At one point we had to move aside to let another recovering patient pass by. We completed a lap and an hour later my nurse came by with some good news, "Dr. Cappatani says you can go home now."

"Where is he? I was hoping to talk to him."

"He was summoned for an emergency surgery. I'm sure he'll be in touch with you."

"Hmmm . . . Okay."

"You can get dressed now, then let me know when you're ready to leave."

I thanked my nurse and then Yukiko left to get me some Tylenol at the pharmacy before driving over to the patient pick-up area. I discarded my hospital gown, grimaced when I ripped off a few residual EKG patches from my hairy chest, and then gingerly put on my clothes. I pushed the call button for my nurse, and she arranged for an orderly to come get me.

*Thirty minutes later the orderly wheeled me down some hallways, into an elevator, then down some more hallways, being sure to jar me at every seam in the floor, until I was outside and free. He stopped at Yukiko's car and said, "Have a nice day, and I hope I never have to see you again." I nodded and smiled and eased myself into the car, starting the rest of my life with only one kidney.*

This is where I go on to describe how Haruto, upon showering after getting home, noticed four small incisions from the laparoscopy on the right side of his abdomen, not on the left. How his gut suddenly hurt more than ever after that discovery. How his future would entail the removal of the cancerous kidney and dialysis until a kidney donor could be found. How he spent hours and hours during dialysis on his laptop trying to find a kidney donor and coordinating with his lawyer about the litigation against the hospital and Dr. Cappatani. And finally, how Dr. Cappatani was found to have ties with the Italian Mafia.

2

The second potential masterpiece attempts to promote philosophical thinking:

*A chicken bone on the ground. More precisely, a KFC chicken wing swarming with ravenous ants on an urban sidewalk. The ants haul away bits of meat along a serpentine trail ending in a long strip of green grass. The chicken and the ants, they are but cogs in the circle of life, where nature takes and gives back life. They are merely two points on the vast circle. Points of scavenger and carrion, predator and prey, feast and famine, luck and fate. Where does the circle start, and where does the circle end?*

*Cluckers the chicken was raised on a dairy farm in northern Idaho.* This is where I go on to describe the life of Cluckers and his subsequent butchering and shipment to KFC.

*Henry's parents were killed in a tragic washing machine accident.* This is where I go on to describe Henry's upbringing at the orphanage, which leads to the dramatic, thought-provoking ending that ties everything together:

*Henry tosses a gnawed KFC chicken wing out the car window, end over end like a Janikowski kickoff. The chicken wing strikes an urban sidewalk and bounces to a stop. A chicken bone on the ground. The circle is complete.*

**17**

# *JEOPARDY ROUND*

This final chapter is a compilation of random things in the following categories:

**Family**

**Pets**

**Potpourri**

**Signs**

**Home Improvement and Maintenance**

**Leisure Time**

Alex[36] reads the answers and Bruce responds with the questions. Let's begin.

---

Category: Signs for $200

Answer: "A clever sign along the road by your house offered this strange item for free."

Question: "What is a dead deer?"

Alex: "Correct! Sounds like a good way to reduce the animal control budget for retrieving roadkill."

Total money: $200

---

Category: Pets for $200

Answer: "This animal gnawed on the placenta from your neighbor's pregnant cow."

Question: "Who is our dog Kip after running away?"

Alex: "Correct! And give that dog more Alpo."

Total money: $400

---

Category: Pets for $400

Answer: "The headless chicken shown here performs this vital job."

Question: "What is lifeguard for our dog Mandu in his wading pool?"

Alex: "Correct! Did Mandu decapitate the chicken?"

Bruce: "Yes, the chicken blew his whistle one too many times."

Total money: $800

---

Category: Signs for $400

Answer: "The sign shown here indicates this."

Question: "What is your left leg will disintegrate if you get too close to a golfer?"

Alex: "Correct! Did you draw this lame stick figure?"

Bruce: "I'm not sure, I need to check the old scraps of paper in the Pictionary box."

Total money $1,200

---

Category: Family for $200

Answer: "This person suddenly fell down while listening to the tennis instructor, then scrambled like a bug to get up off her back before anyone noticed."

Question: "Who is my wife Karen?"

Alex: "No, you fool! It was Karen's mom, and Karen almost wet herself laughing while the rest of the class went to help her mom."

Total money: $1,000

---

Category: Family for $400

Answer: "Your mom once lost it with you when you were a toddler and did this."

Question: "What is smash a tuna sandwich in my face after I nagged her incessantly for it?"

Alex: "Correct! And you got what you deserved."

Total money: $1,400

---

Category: Family for $600

Answer: "Your son Joel had this embarrassment while listening to a park ranger's somber presentation at Antietam National Battlefield about the bloodiest day in American history."

Question: "What is he farted?"

Alex: "No, you crude bastard! What is his cell phone rang."

Total money: $800

---

Category: Family for $800

Answer: "Your son Matt earned the nickname "Sweet Cheeks" for doing this."

Question: "What is chew a 10-piece wad of Bazooka bubble gum?"

Alex: "No, you imbecile! What is sit down on the couch to watch the ninth inning of a Giants-Dodgers game and send good vibes to the Giants who made a dramatic comeback to beat the Dodgers."

Total money: $0

---

Category: Family for $1,000

Answer: "This person fell into a pond while walking in the dark back to the car."

Question: "Who is my dad?"

Alex: "Correct!"

Bruce: "And the sight of him soaked with algae hanging from his face made my mom wet her pants."

Total money: $1,000

---

Category: Pets for $600

Answer: "Your dog Mandu is shown here doing this."

Question: "What is raising his injured paw after stepping on a thistle?"

Alex: "No, you ignoramus! What is assuming the gopher hole attack position."

Total money: $400

---

Category: Pets for $800

Answer: "Your dog Mandu is shown here doing this."

Question: "What is pooping?"

Alex: "Correct! Note the same intensity as in the previous picture, albeit the focus is on a different hole."

Total money: $1,200

---

Category: Home Improvement and Maintenance for $200

Answer: "While building your carport this unfortunate incident occurred."

Question: "What is the roof collapsed onto our brand-new Tesla Roadster?"

Alex: "Wrong, and you can't afford a Tesla! What is

a spark from the metal saw started a grass fire on your neighbor's property."

Total money: $1,000

---

Category: Home Improvement and Maintenance for $400

Answer: "The 5-foot-long object shown here is this."

Question: "What is a snake or a dreadlock?"

Alex: "Can you be more specific?"

Modified Question: "What is a snake?"

Alex: "Wrong again! What is an enormous root mass that was removed from an irrigation pipe."

Total money: $600

---

Category: Home Improvement and Maintenance for $600

Answer: "The disaster shown here was caused by this."

Question: "What is our house painter?"

Alex: "Judges? We'll accept that but we were looking for what is a wind storm."

Total money: $1,200

Category: Leisure Time for $200

Answer: "While horseback riding in Idaho your guide stopped to do this."

Question: "What is pop off the head of an injured bird as casually as popping off a champagne cork?"

Alex: "Correct! It must have been the humane thing to do."

Total money: $1,400

Category: Leisure Time for $400

Answer: "These priceless reactions were triggered by the ride shown here."

Question: "What is the rocket blastoff ride on top of the Stratosphere in Las Vegas?"

Alex: "Correct!"

Bruce: "And you can see that I'm about to pass out, Karen has pulled a neck muscle, and Joel is transfixed on the ground. Matt wisely declined to get on the ride."

Total money: $1,800

Category: Leisure Time for $600

Answer: "Museums are much more enjoyable to experience when these are present."

Question: "What are video displays so I don't have to read so many of those informative placards?"

Alex: "Correct, you lazy bastard!"

Total money: $2,400

Category: Potpourri for $200

Answer: "Karen considers a gas tank to be half full, others consider it to be half empty, but engineers consider it to be this."

Question: "What is overdesigned?"

Alex: "Correct, you damn engineer! Have you ever run out of gas?"

Bruce: "Yes, twice."

Total money: $2,600

Category: Potpourri for $400

Answer: "This Father's Day present went missing in the car and led to accusations against all family members."

Question: "What is a tie?"

Alex: "No, that's boring! What is a blueberry truffle."

Bruce: "And it was never found. Perhaps taking stool samples could have solved the mystery."

Total money: $2,200

Category: Signs for $600

Answer: "The sign shown here indicates this."

Question: "What is on my street you can't plug in an electric appliance?"

Alex: "No, you delusional idiot! What is you must turn around to leave Shaffer Street."

Total money: $1,600

---

Category: Signs for $800

Answer: "The sign shown here indicates this."

Question: "What is a man-eating monster with a pointed tail is present?"

Alex: "No, and your imagination sucks! What is breaking waves are present."

Total money: $800

---

Category: Signs for $1,000

Answer: "The sign shown here indicates this."

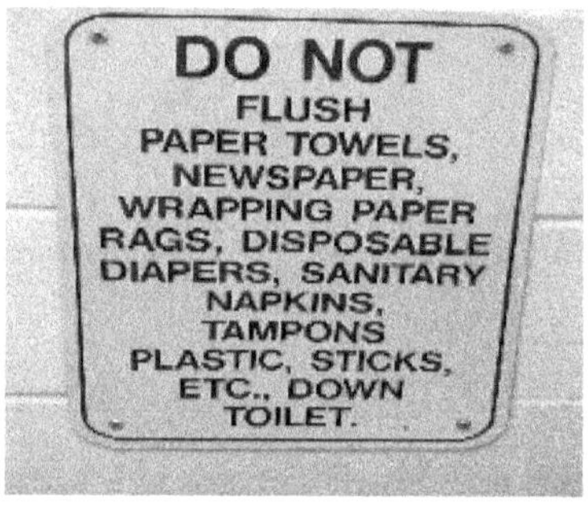


Question: "What is people are stupid?"

Alex: "Correct! What is the 'ETC.?'"

Bruce: "I'm thinking extra tall chickens."

Total money: $1,800

---

Category: Potpourri for $600

Answer: "A man at the Baseball Hall of Fame in Cooperstown, New York took your picture for this reason."

Question: "What is he thought I was hall-of-famer John Smoltz?"

Alex: "Correct!"

Bruce: "And I thought about charging him five bucks for an autograph."

Total money: $2,400

---

Category: Pets for $1,000

Answer: "Your pet goat turned purple for this reason."

Question: "What is he blushed?"

Alex: "No, you dimwit! What is he was rubbed with blackberries."

Bruce: "That would be the work of Joel."

Total money: $1,400

---

Category: Home Improvement and Maintenance for $800

Answer: "This has happened twice as a result of burning your debris pile."

Question: "What is firemen have come to issue a warning about too much smoke?"

Alex: "Correct!"

Bruce: "And I'd really like to know which neighbor called to complain about the smoke."

Total money: $2,200

---

Category: Potpourri for $800

Answer: "Your friend Jack from Arizona has this unique collection."

Question: "What is a cactus collection?"

Alex: "No, you moron! What is an airlines barf bag collection."

Bruce: "And they're empty."

Total money: $1,400

Category: Potpourri for $1,000

Answer: "Karen hears this ringtone when you call her."

Question: "What is Lynyrd Skynyrd's *Simple Man?*"

Alex: "Correct!"

Bruce: "I'd like to think I'm a simple man."

Total money: $2,400

Category: Leisure Time for $800

Answer: "This person had a photo collection of dog poop piles."

Question: "Who is someone with a special sense of humor?"

Alex: "Can you be more specific?"

Modified Question: "Who is Karen's dad?"

Alex: "Correct! Remember, beauty is in the eye of the beholder."

Total money: $3,200

---

Category: Leisure Time for $1,000

Answer: "This happened when you skied the blue course at Alpine Meadows Ski Resort near Lake Tahoe."

Question: "What is I finished on the red course?"

Alex: "Correct!"

Bruce: "Yep, finished on my butt with a chorus of mock cheers."

Total money: $4,200

---

Category: Home Improvement and Maintenance for $1,000

Answer: "Your neighbor did this to locate a leak in your pipe on her property."

Question: "What is crank up the water and flood her property?"

Alex: "Wrong yet again! What is use a witching rod."

Bruce: "And it didn't work."

Total money: $3,200

---

## FINAL JEOPARDY

Category: Dave Barry

Wager: All of it.

Answer: "This page of Dave Barry's *Live Right and Find Happiness* states, "Every time you turn on the TV, there's David Beckham in Woo Mode, attending government functions, meeting with civic groups, talking with students, rescuing babies from alligators, stopping hurricanes with his bare hands and just generally being handsome and charming and hugely popular in the greater Miami area."

Question: "You've got to be freakin' kidding me!"

Alex: "Be sure to phrase your response in the form of a question."

Modified Question: "What is you've got to be freakin' kidding me?"

Alex: "Pick a number, any number."

Revised Modified Question: "What is 102?"

Alex: "No, and you finish with nothing! You loser! What is page 22. I certainly hope you have better luck in the game of life. See you next time on Jeopardy!"

Total money: $0

# EPILOGUE

It started with a pickle crock, but how will it end? In death of course. Should I preserve my 8-month baby brain cryonically on that sad, heartbreaking, tragic day when I check out? No, let's get that out of the way right now. What do I hope to accomplish and experience in my remaining years? Now that's a thought-provoking question.

I hope to be more like Forrest Gump, accomplishing and experiencing many of the things that he did. In some ways I'm already like Forrest Gump, I was good at football and ping pong, I could run pretty fast after discarding my "magic shoes," I'm an awkward dancer, and I like chocolates.

But Forrest Gump did so much more. I hope to:

1. be a good public speaker like he was at the Lincoln Memorial Reflection Pool.

2. read *Curious George*[37] to a grandchild as well-behaved and cute as his son, "Little Forrest."

3. ride my bike across the country and see beautiful scenery like when he ran across the country.

4. do random acts of kindness like he did helping Vivian Malone with her dropped books as she confronted Governor George Wallace to enroll at the University of Alabama.

5. be able to converse easily with total strangers like he did at the Savannah bus stop.

6. always enjoy ice cream as much as he did at the army hospital in Vietnam.

7. be a loyal friend like he was with Jenny, Bubba, and Lieutenant Dan.

8. excel at writing like he excelled at putting together his army rifle.

9. take a chance on something like he did by buying a shrimp boat.

10. be a generous philanthropist like he was for Bubba's family.

11. be a successful investor like he was by investing in Apple early.

12. maintain the outside of my house as immaculate as he maintained the Gump House.

13. be a good caregiver like he was for his mom and Jenny.

If I can do these things, and have my sons change my diaper, I will have lived a rich, full life.

# FOOTNOTES

1. Metal antennae.

2. Tall metal backrests.

3. Homemade wooden race cars.

4. Woodley Island station, 1942-2017.

5. Looking up these shows on your smartphones, you'll see that *Wild Wild West* was a science fiction western series with two Secret Service agents who had a large array of gizmos to solve crimes during President Grant's administration. *Adam-12* was a drama that followed two police officers as they rode the streets of Los Angeles in their patrol car.

6. Insert your favorite explosion onomatopoeia here.

7. Running naked in a public place. Perhaps the most famous streak was at the 1974 Oscars. While David Niven was introducing Elizabeth Taylor, a streaker raced past him flashing a peace sign.

8. i.

9. 1976 boxing movie starring Sylvester Stallone that won the Academy Award for Best Picture.

10. A device that spins a record (vinyl disk) at 33, 45, or 78 rpms and reproduces music when a needle (stylus) vibrates traveling over grooves in the record and the vibrations are amplified.

11. A dime was actually worth something back then.

12. Photoshop didn't exist.

13. The views and opinions expressed are those of the author and do not necessarily reflect the official policy or position of reality.

14. 1985 science fiction movie starring Michael J. Fox as Marty McFly who accidentally travels back in time to 1955 where he meets his future parents.

15. Australian-born American actor who achieved world-wide fame for his romantic swashbuckler roles in Hollywood films.

16. The ballpark before AT&T Park, which is now Oracle Park.

17. An old-fashioned DVD.

18. An old-fashioned DVD player.

19. Also embarrassing music for injured high school football players returning to the field.

20. Pay phones were operated by depositing coins.

21. An estimate is something you do when you don't have Google Maps.

22. Uh, I suppose the picture could have been altered.

23. Uncle Ben's Rice, the top-selling rice in the U.S. from 1950 to the 1990s.

24. D.B. Cooper hijacked a Boeing 727 in the airspace between Portland, Oregon and Seattle, Washington on the afternoon of November 24, 1971. He extorted $200,000 in ransom at the Seattle-Tacoma airport and took to the air again, only to parachute with the money to an uncertain fate.

25. Thus restoring my faith in Millennials.

26. Check YouTube for a clip of the famous crooning.

27. Check YouTube for a Real Men of Genius ad, and

if you're really ambitious you can sing along with my lyrics instead of theirs.

28. The sitcom *Frasier* was broadcast from 1993 to 2004 and featured psychiatrist Dr. Frasier Crane (Kelsey Grammer).

29. 1994 movie starring Tim Robbins as banker Andy Dufresne who is sentenced to life in Shawshank State Penitentiary for the murder of his wife and her lover despite his claims of innocence.

30. Mighty Mouse was an animated superhero mouse that first appeared in 1942.

31. 1960 psychological horror movie directed by Alfred Hitchcock and starring Anthony Perkins and Janet Leigh.

32. 1974 mystery inspired by the California water wars starring Jack Nicholson and Faye Dunaway.

33. 1989 comedy directed by Ron Howard about family and parenting experiences.

34. Either of the two corners of a boxing ring not used by the boxers and their handlers.

35. Sung like "I'm Popeye the sailor man," the last line of Popeye's theme song, including the two toots on his corncob pipe at the end.

36. Alex Trebekstonbergermanjansenhan (to avoid a libel suit).

37. A series of popular children's books originating in 1941 featuring a chimpanzee orphan brought from Africa to a giant city by "The Man with the Yellow Hat."

Also by Bruce Shaffer

The Man with the Yellowfin Tuna
The Bonnacon Goes to Calgary
The Bonnacon Goes to Pamplona
The Final Play
A Goat's Life
The Folsom Rewind

# ABOUT THE AUTHOR

Bruce Shaffer has written feature magazine stories and sports articles for publications near his adopted hometown of Folsom, California. As a civil engineer, he authored many water resources documents during his 26-year career. Now retired, Bruce enjoys tapping into his life experiences and creativity to compose works of non-fiction and fiction, including his humorous personal memoirs, *It Started with a Pickle Crock*. He lives happily with his wonderful wife, a playful dog, and a defiant cat, and has two awesome grown sons in Northern California.